CHANGE

count on it

death,

faith &

miracles

by bill mcDonald with kirk noonan

CHANGE count on it

Change: *Count On It*
By Bill McDonald
with Kirk Noonan

Printed in the United States of America
ISBN: 978-0-615-28428-6
Copyright 2009, Bill McDonald and Simpleplan Media. *simpleplan media*

Design by Marc McBride
Production by Lucas Key

Unless otherwise indicated, all Scripture references are from the Holy
Bible: New International Version, copyright 1984, Zondervan Bible
Publishers.

This book is based on fact, but some elements are fictionalized.

DEDICATION

*To **my heroes** — Seth, Leah, Joil, Drew, Will and Emelia —*
who just happen to be my kids. To my wife of my youth,
Connie, who still is the love and joy of my life. And to
Him who is worthy of all praise.

Ken,
Thank you for
believing in us.

Bill

CHANGE count on it

contents

ENDORSEMENTS

Bill and Connie McDonald are veteran missionaries who epitomize vision, faith and accomplishment. After establishing a Bible school, Christian school and a powerful 3,000-member congregation, they accepted the daunting challenge of pioneering a family-values television network for the Spanish-speaking world. As a member of the founding board of Unsión Television, I have watched as Bill and Connie have accepted the challenges and encountered the obstacles in establishing Unsión. When the fire destroyed the studios, it was their vision, faith, passion and endurance that brought them through this disaster and set the stage for even greater ministry. Their clear vision and steadfast faith continue to inspire and guide the Unsión team through turbulent economic times and the challenges of a growing television ministry that touches most of the Americas and part of Europe. Millions are receiving a gospel witness, and close to 40,000 have come to faith in Jesus through this television ministry. Bill and Connie's passion for souls and pioneer missionary spirit are distinguishing them as great missionary leaders in the world today.

David Lee
Director of U.S. Relations
Assemblies of God World Missions

This is the story of an amazing journey covering thousands of miles, crossing oceans, continents, time zones, political arenas and digital cyberspace. It's the fabric of life, love and passion for not just making an impact, but making a difference. This is the journey...of a lifetime.

Joe Girdler
Superintendent, Kentucky District

Thirteen years ago I met Bill McDonald. Immediately, I learned that he was a man with a rare combination of vision, passion and commitment. I have seen him at moments of triumph and of great challenge. I have seen him encourage and inspire men and women to aspire to greater heights than they knew they could achieve. I have seen him pushed to the limits of human ability only to find new strength in God. No matter the setback or challenge, Bill has persevered in order to accomplish what God has planned for him. His story is one that will encourage and inspire you.

Mark Lehmann
Pastor, Cornerstone AG, Bowie, Maryland
Asst. Superintendent, Potomac District

The Gulf Latin American District of the Assemblies of God strongly supports Unsión Television because we believe it to be an effective way to reach into the lives of individuals and families. Unsión's unique programming is not only an excellent tool to directly present the message of the gospel, but it also effectively illustrates how the gospel is lived out in a person's daily life. Through stories that present the Christian worldview and values, Unsión Television is a powerful influence throughout the Spanish-speaking world that promotes faith in God and the Christian lifestyle, which in turn positively affects families, communities and the world.

Gary Jones
Superintendent, Gulf Latin American District
San Antonio, Texas

Every now and then it happens — we launch something beyond our capacity because we've heard from God. The blessings come, but along with it, challenges bigger than we ever imagined, and the temptation is to believe it really wasn't a God-thing after all . . . and then — it happens! Something so unmistakable that we take a step back, regroup in our spirit, and say, "Surely God is in this!"

And we have strength, supernatural strength, to go on because God is in it!

That's what is happening with Unsión Television, perhaps the most unique television network ever. It is family-values-based television potentially reaching out to the secular communities of the 500 million Spanish speakers in the world!

But it is more than just wholesome television programming. It also airs two hours of daily gospel programming and periodic 30-second spots designed to encourage desperate people to call in to a local number for Christian counseling. Since its beginning, over 100,000 people have called Un Buen Consejo (Good Advice), and about half of them have accepted Christ and are being discipled. Tremendous!

This is what Unsión is all about: changing society and changing lives.

Richard Nicholson
Regional Director, Latin America and the Caribbean
Assemblies of God World Missions

CHANGE count on it

FOREWORD

Where do you turn when the changes of life are so great and insurmountable that everything seems hopeless?

If you're anything like my good friends and colleagues, Bill and Connie McDonald, you turn to God.

In writing this foreword, I pinned down three important lessons Bill and Connie's lives convey: First, no matter the circumstance or report, one must hang onto any shred of hope — even if it is only a thread. Second, life's tragedies and setbacks demand that we put complete trust in Jesus Christ. Third, when thrust into hopeless situations, followers of Christ should give unrelenting praise and thanks to God.

Admittedly, this kind of living runs against the grain. In fact, such actions won't always make sense. But time and time again I have seen Bill and Connie deal with seemingly hopeless situations in such a way. And each time they have prevailed.

In *Change: Count On It*, you'll walk with Bill and Connie as they receive devastating news about their newborn children. You'll also visit the aftermath of a tragic fire that almost ended their ministry. Through such setbacks you'll learn how this remarkable missionary couple to Ecuador has remained grounded in their faith while staring hopelessness in the face.

Since serving in Ecuador, Bill and Connie have planted churches, ministered to untold thousands and founded Unsión — a television network that has the ability to reach every Spanish-speaking country in the world. They've done so with excellence, but also at a great price and much sacrifice.

Bill and Connie are stubborn people who live to rely on God. Because of it, God has transformed one hopeless situation after the next into a victory for them.

Since they founded Unsión, literally thousands of people have committed to become followers of Christ. Recently, I asked Bill how a couple with no prior television industry experience could found and operate such a powerful tool for the gospel. He smiled and admitted it had nothing to do with him.

"We just learned early on that the way to influence culture and lead people to a relationship with Jesus was to tell them powerful stories," he said. "Doing that changes culture and lives."

Like most things Bill does, he does not stay within conventional bounds for a television network with a Christian worldview.

Unsión produces and broadcasts cooking, news and biblically based teaching programs. The ministry plans to produce and broadcast a soap opera that shows the impact of sinful living while pointing people to Jesus. Evangelism takes place several times an hour as each program aired is wedged between explicitly Christian commercial-length spots that tell of Jesus' love, grace and mercy.

In *Change: Count On It*, you'll learn more about Bill and Connie, the Unsión ministry and why Christians should be embracing careers in the media. But more importantly, you'll draw inspiration and be given the tools to face any situation no matter how hopeless it may seem.

A book that can do that for you is well worth reading.

L. John Bueno
Executive Director
Assemblies of God World Missions

ACKNOWLEDGEMENTS

Thanks to all our friends.

INTRODUCTION

I remember clearly the day my dad drove home in a well-worn blue 1954 Ford sedan. The Ford's paint was faded, dings speckled the sides, the engine needed a major overhaul, and the interior was shot.

I loved that car the moment I saw it!

Though the Ford might have looked like a heap to some people, our blue-collar neighbors did not complain. Our car looked a lot like theirs.

Though it would be years before I could legally drive, I regularly climbed behind the Ford's steering wheel and pretended to cruise around my neighborhood and throughout Louisville, Kentucky.

By the time I was 12, I must have put at least a 100,000 miles on that car without ever starting the engine. My dad did not mind me playing in the car, and I often stretched my legs as far as I could, pushed in the clutch and mercilessly shifted the gears.

I was so amazed to see how seasoned drivers could shift through the gears without missing one word of an ongoing conservation with other passengers in the car. Heck, my dad could shift from second to third, backhand a couple of unruly kids, carry on a conversation with my mom and not miss a beat. It was obvious; learning to manage the change of gears was key to getting to any destination.

Behind the wheel of that old Ford was one of my favorite places. But it was not until a terrible day in my adulthood that

I realized how similar life was to my playtime in the Ford.

In 1981 I stood in an intensive care unit. Tears rolled down my cheeks as my eyes were set on my newborn son. Somehow I could not find my breath, I could not find my faith. It should have been a momentous occasion, but it was anything but that. Billy needed a miracle. Interestingly, it was at that moment the old Ford came to mind. I had learned as a kid how to make the necessary changes in that old Ford; now, could I apply that lesson to my present crisis?

That is what this book is all about — *CHANGE*. Change happens to all of us. Sometimes we cause it, and at times it is thrust upon us. Sometimes it is good and wonderful, and at other times it is unpleasant and seemingly insurmountable.

I have experienced the Lord's guidance in my personal and professional lives time and time again. He walked me through the necessary changes as I grappled with Billy's condition a quarter of a century ago, and He is walking with me today as I attempt to use television to change the culture for Jesus Christ.

Though change is inevitable and always fraught with risk, it offers unprecedented opportunity that we, as followers of Christ, can seize if we will allow God to walk before us. No matter what the circumstance, great things await those who put their hope in God.

It is my prayer that our story and the story of the Unsión Television will prove that to you.

— *Bill McDonald*

ESTROYED

cuenca,
ecuador
2006

Menacing plumes of black smoke poured out of the building as colorful flames devoured the structure. As the fire raced through the building, employees fled for their lives. Like all disasters do, ours attracted onlookers. Though I was not there to see it myself, those onlookers were witness to the loss of hundreds of thousands of dollars, numerous years of hard work, countless sacrifices and many dreams.

I am glad I was not there.

Had I been, I probably would have rushed in like a madman and tried to extinguish the flames myself. After all, the destruction of the Unsión studios in Cuenca, Ecuador, was the day my long-held vision to bring Christian-values television to Ecuadorians turned into a pile of rubble and ash.

"How did it start?" I blurted into my cell phone to Carlos Gonzalez, administrative director of the network, who had the unfortunate task of letting me know about the fire.

"I don't know," Carlos said, his voice, steady, yet somber. "A welder was working on the roof and suddenly the studios were burning down."

Carlos was working off limited information too. It would have been impossible for him to have all the answers I was looking for. But since I was 2,000 miles away in the United States doing fund-raising for Unsión, I could not help but want to know everything about the fire.

"Is everyone all right?"

Again, Carlos did not know.

"Pastor Bill, I'll call you back when I know more," he finally promised. "But you need to get back to Ecuador as soon as possible."

Three years of toiling to build a Christian television ministry had gone up in flames, and there was not a thing I could do about it — except talk to God.

"This is over," I cried out to Him. "Everything we've worked so hard for is gone in less than 10 minutes. What a waste. I can't do it again. I'm sorry, I just can't."

As I prayed, many memories came rushing back. I could not help but think of all the sacrifices faithful Ecuadorians and Americans had made to build Unsión. Work teams from the United States had come down consistently. Generous donors had provided finances. On countless Sundays, I found wedding bands and jewelry in the offering buckets. Members of our congregation who did not have a dime to spare wanted so badly to be a part of building the facilities and ministry that they gave their prized possessions.

"Lord, why did this happen?" I asked, trying hard to keep the rising anger within me from spilling over into my conversation with God.

As I grappled with the question, my friend Peter came to mind. Peter was a young man in our church who wanted nothing more than to serve others. Instantly, in my estimation, his sacrifice for our church and Unsión seemed the greatest.

He had planted a daughter church in an indigenous community in the heart of the Andes Mountains and was nearing the completion of his studies at our Bible institute. Always one to serve, Peter did not hesitate to volunteer when he learned there were some adjustments needed to the tiles on the roof at our church in Cuenca.

Eager to help, he climbed onto the roof. But while doing repairs he slipped and fell to his death. At his funeral his mother approached me. With tears of frustration and looking for someone to feel her pain she began pounding on my chest.

"Why did you send Peter onto that roof?" she cried. "He was my oldest son. Why did you send him on the roof? Why, why, why?"

I was at a loss for words. Somehow the pounding of her small fists against my chest was comforting. I felt guilty and deserving of everything she could dish out. My heart went out to her, but I did not have an explanation as to why her son — a very good, God-fearing young man with unlimited potential — had died. All I could think of at the time was that he had made the ultimate sacrifice in helping build the church where Unsión was birthed.

I sensed Peter's mother was not consolable at the time, so I took the physical and verbal blows without resistance.

offerings

As thoughts of the fire competed with memories of all the sacrifices I had witnessed over the years, I was overwhelmed with tears. It was as if a tsunami of pain and grief had slammed down on me. Once again, unexpected change had caught me off guard. But before I succumbed to the crushing blows, I felt God speak something into my soul.

"This fire did not take Me by surprise."

As those words trickled through my being, the sense of hopelessness that threatened to consume me once again suddenly lifted, and my mind became clear.

Nothing — not even unexpected, insurmountable changes — takes God by surprise. It was another life-changing epiphany — good and bad never take God by surprise. The thought amazed me.

Suddenly, March 27, 2006, did not have to be a day the work God had us doing in Ecuador came to an end. Instead, the change that came that day could be the fresh start God could use to transform the ministry and us in ways we never imagined — all we had to do was let Him. After all, the fire did not take Him by surprise, so why should I move forward pretending it did?

I grabbed my cell phone and started making calls. Within a few hours I had booked a flight back to Ecuador.

Knowing God was not taken by surprise gave me the fuel I needed to take charge. Everything was going to be OK, I was sure of that. I had to be. People were depending on me.

I flew to Ecuador with the expectation God would use the tragedy to do something greater than I could have ever imagined.

But after landing in Cuenca and rushing to what was left of our studios, I could not believe what I saw. Nothing would ever be the same. And at that moment, I was not sure if that was a good or bad thing.

At Unsión
we believe in the power of stories

A few years ago I took my daughter, Leah, and son, Seth, camping. Our goal was to hike Cotopaxi, a volcano in the Andes Mountains, which happens to be the highest active volcano in the world.

After our first day of hiking we bunked in a primitive cabin. Like whipped puppies we crawled into our sleeping bags.

"Daddy, tell us a story," said Leah, who is now married and has three children of her own.

"Did I ever tell you about your Great-Grandpa Fink?" I asked, more than willing to tell a story.

In the cold and dark of the cabin I spun a yarn about Grandpa Fink. Before I knew it, Leah and Seth were giggling and sharing their own funny stories.

Our stories joined other memories from our hiking expedition that weekend, and I figured they would be lost in the mix of our volcano adventure. But a couple of months later, I heard Seth telling someone about his amazing Great-Grandpa Fink.

Time and time again I have had the opportunity to share stories of my dad, Bill, and how he labored with his hands. It seemed from my earliest recollection that there was nothing he could not build or repair. From a shabby artificial Christmas tree to the overhaul of a '54 Ford, he had the tools and wisdom to fix anything that did not work. Somehow I believe that these stories have helped shape the work ethic I see in my children today.

At Unsión we believe in the power of stories, and it is our conviction that as followers of Christ we need to be the best at telling them.

Stories of hope, faith and love allow us to identify with models and examples of courage and virtue. Stories remind us of who we are and give us a better understanding of why we are here and why our lives are important.

When I first met Dick Givan, my wife's dad, I quickly sized him up as a man's man. The fading blue ink of tattoos stretched across each arm quietly told of his years as a sailor.

"I was on a Landing Ship Tank in World War II," he told me when I inquired about the tattoos. "We went through seven invasions. I was a gunner's mate…"

As he spoke, I allowed myself to join him in the past. His descriptions were so good I could almost hear the scream of artillery overhead. In my mind's eye, I could almost see him as a young, wide-eyed sailor soaked in sweat as he scrambled to load his assigned weapon.

During a major invasion, he went on, the gun under his command blazed, but suddenly froze. He explained that he had loaded the shell, but when he pulled the trigger the only reply he got was a dull click — a faulty round in the chamber.

"We all knew that round could explode at any moment," my father-in-law said. "We needed all guns operational."

He then made the critical choice to risk everything, open the gun, pull out the shell and dump it overboard. Doing so was risky business. As the shell dropped to the sea below, he said, it felt as if an eternity passed.

"Just as it went into the ocean, it exploded," recalled my father-in-law. "Scared me. I guess I should've run and left it, but I stayed."

He was not boasting. Instead, he was reminding himself that men must be men of courage and must stay and do what needs to be done when everything in them is telling them to abandon their post and look out for themselves.

Other underlying elements that ran through the stories Dick told were his expectations he had for me and the four other guys who would eventually marry his daughters. I think his strategy worked — Connie and I have been married for more than 30 years.

My dad's and Dick's ability to lace themes and expectations into their stories is something we strive to do at Unsión. As followers of Christ, we actively engage culture with stories that will make a difference.

FORMED

uisville,
entucky
1969

The lights were dimmed, but the mirrored disco ball spinning in the center of the roller-skating rink provided just enough light for me to spot her. She was standing with her friends, and I assumed she was waiting for a boy to ask her to dance.

Lynn and I went to the same high school and were in the same grade. Though I did not know her well, I had spoken to her on occasion. That was good enough for me, so I took a deep breath and strode across the rink with James Taylor's "Fire and Rain" booming over the antiquated sound system.

As I approached Lynn, she smiled shyly at me. I leaned in and asked if she wanted to dance. She said something in response, but the music was so loud I could not hear a word she said. What I did notice immediately was her head moving from right to left. The all-American, nonverbal cue for the word no. I leaned in again, anyway.

"I can't hear you," I shouted.

"I have a boyfriend."

"Oh, a boyfriend. So you probably can't dance."

She nodded.

I contemplated my next move. But Lynn leaned toward me this time.

"Why don't you ask my little sister to dance?" She pointed to the cute girl standing next to her. I did not know her, but I wanted to dance.

"Do you want to dance?" I asked.

Lynn's little sister smiled and nodded. I grabbed her hand and led her to the middle of the dance floor.

"I'm Billy, by the way."

"I'm Connie," she said shyly, but loudy enough so I could hear. "Thanks for asking me to dance."

"No problem."

A few nights later I took Connie to Dairy Queen, bought her an ice cream cone and began to fall in love. She was only 14 — two years younger than I was — but I didn't care. She intrigued me the moment I met her.

After our little trip to Dairy Queen, Connie's mom informed me that her daughter was too young to date. But, she added, she would allow me to pick Connie up from work and take her back home. Not exactly what I had in mind, but the rule wound up being providential.

called

Connie had landed a job working at an Assemblies of God church that was only a few blocks from her home. Though her family did not attend the church, Connie got the job because the church was desperate for help in their nursery.

One Sunday evening I sauntered into the church to pick up Connie. I was early, so I started looking around the lobby somewhat intrigued. Immediately, I noticed the church was very different from the Roman Catholic church I had grown up in. Hearing singing emanating from the sanctuary, and not wanting to hang out in an empty lobby, I decided to attend the church's "mass," figuring it was similar to the ones at my church.

As soon as I pulled open the sanctuary doors to get a peek inside, I was greeted by the sweet sounds of praise and prayer. I craned my neck to get a good look. As I surveyed the throng of worshippers, I noticed they all looked happy and even glad to be in church.

With my curiosity more piqued, I stepped into the sanctuary as the doors silently closed behind me. If my eyes were not betraying me, people had their hands raised and their bodies were swaying. This was too much. I had never seen anything like this before. As I continued to look around, I noticed that some of the worshippers even had tears running down their faces.

Seeing people worship in such a way shocked my senses. Though unnerved by what I was experiencing, I never thought of leaving. Instead, I made my way to an empty pew and found a seat to watch more of the show.

Raised in a Catholic home, I was taught to fear God, love my neighbor and work hard and honestly. Since childhood I had admired those qualities and tried hard to do such things to the best of my ability. However, my teen years proved corrosive to that foundation as I had a habit of making poor choices. But that night, as I sat in the sanctuary, I quickly found myself inspired by the words of the pastor.

For reasons I could not comprehend at the time, I was suddenly keenly interested in learning all I could about the things of God. Even stranger to me was that I felt a stirring in my soul that was completely foreign.

"The Lord is coming again," proclaimed the pastor as he stood behind the pulpit. "And when He does, every believer in Him will be swept into the air. It will be a glorious day when the Church experiences the Rapture."

The Rapture? Huh?

I had never heard such a message in my life. It excited and scared me simultaneously. Goose bumps rose on my arms as the pastor, W.L. Rodgers, asked for eyes to be closed and heads bowed at the close of the service.

"If you don't want to miss out on the Rapture, you need to ask Jesus Christ to be your Lord and Savior," Rodgers almost whispered into his microphone. "Jesus died for your sins. All you have to do is confess them and ask Jesus to be the Lord of your life. Is there anyone tonight who wants to make that commitment?"

I felt my hand go up. I figured if that's all I had to do to get into heaven I was going to do it.

"I see that hand, thank you," said the pastor. "I see that one too, thank you."

Getting saved, as Christians called it, and having a guarantee that I was going to heaven was proving easy. It was exactly the kind of change I needed.

"Now, folks, if you raised your hands, I want you to come down to these altars." The pastor had left the pulpit by this point and was now down in front of the first row of the congregation.

He waved his hand as if to direct all of us who had raised our hands to come to him. "Come on down to the altars if you raised your hand. God has something special for you tonight."

I could feel my mind whirring and red flags going up warning me not to go forward. With every ounce of me I wanted to resist the invitation. After all, who wants to be made a spectacle during a service where he or she does not know anyone? Despite my misgivings, I went forward and found myself kneeling at the altar.

I had no plans of attending service that night or responding to a sermon, and I especially did not have any desire to go in front of a bunch of people I did not know to do something I was just learning about. But before I knew it, I was taking part in another tradition I had no knowledge of.

"For all of you who came forward, I want you to repeat after me," Rodgers said. "Dear Jesus, forgive me of my sins."

I repeated what Rodgers said.

"Be the Lord of my life. I want to accept You as my Savior."

I did not hesitate to say that either.

When Rodgers had finished praying and I had finished repeating his every word, I suddenly felt a peace I'd never known. Something had definitely changed within me.

As the music played I continued to pray. It was an incredibly peaceful experience. The singing of the worshippers filled the air, and I realized it was the first time in my life I had truly felt the presence of God.

After several minutes I opened my eyes and found Connie kneeling beside me. I learned later that someone had dashed to the nursery when they saw me go forward and informed her that her date had gone down to the altar to accept Jesus.

When Connie, who was raised Baptist but had never committed her life to Christ, heard I had gone forward she raced to the sanctuary and accepted Christ too.

While we prayed that night I also felt called to ministry, though I had no idea what that would entail.

Looking back now, I realize Connie and I did not have a clue about the journey we were embarking on. It was the kind of journey that would continue to transform and challenge us to a newer and better way of living.

But it was also the kind of journey that would see us get involved in the church's youth group, be discipled in the Word and prepared for Bible college. It would also prepare us for marriage, ministry, the mission field and the founding of Unsión Television.

Unbeknown to us that night, the journey would also see us through some of the toughest and most agonizing moments of our lives.

We had no idea. All we knew at the time was that we had both fallen in love with Jesus.

At Unsión
we believe stories can
convey the Hope of the world

A few hours outside of Quito, where Unsión is headquartered, are
some of the most beautiful valleys in the world. Lush green jungles
cling to the steep mountains. Gorgeous waterfalls, hundreds of feet tall,
cascade down. Carved into the sides of the mountains are thin, curvy, and
sometimes guardrail-less, roads.

Just the thought of driving, walking or standing near the edge of these
perilous cliffs is scary for many reasons — especially when there are no
guardrails. But when there are guardrails they lend a sense of safety and
peace that has a tendency to keep fear at bay.

Through stories we can lay down boundaries (guardrails) for people in
our circle of influence. The reason? When we tell stories, we plant values
and security in people's lives. This is especially true when it comes to
children. As children grow older, stories help to shape and mold them.
Stories can teach people the difference between right and wrong. When
our stories square with our values they can communicate beliefs and ways
to live to the next generation.

We have a peculiar habit in our home of putting mayonnaise on our
peanut butter sandwiches. We would never think of putting jelly with
peanut butter, only mayonnaise and peanut butter. My children and
grandchildren only eat a peanut butter sandwich with mayonnaise. Three
generations, all eschewing the time-honored PB&J.

I began to wonder how we locked in on that combination. I traced
the practice to Connie, realizing that was how she had always made
sandwiches for our family. But she could not explain why.

So she asked her mom, "Why do we do it like this?"

"Because your dad likes it like that," came the answer.

"Why does Dad put mayonnaise on his peanut butter?"

And with the answer came another story of life-shaping values. During
World War II, Connie's dad and his crewmates would be out to sea for

months at a time. Food aged. The peanut butter and bread got very, very dry. The peanut butter especially, since the cook on that ship pulled the oil off of the peanut butter to use in other foods. So, when sandwiches were made, the cook would spread mayonnaise on the bread, bringing renewed moisture to the bread and softening the dried peanut butter.

Three generations of our family have acquired a taste for this strange concoction. But now when we eat peanut butter with mayonnaise we understand it goes back to principles of loyalty, service, self-sacrifice and love of country.

On a recent visit to my hometown, Seth and Connie and I visited the east end of Louisville, Kentucky, the site of my earliest childhood memories. Our family had lived above Goman's Drugstore next door to Mr. Kessinger and his family.

I had a little friend, just two doors down, and we would play in his front yard. One evening my friend threw a hammer. It happened to catch me in the forehead, claws first. I still have the scars.

Mr. Kessinger was walking by when he saw me crying and bleeding. He was wearing a white shirt and he picked me up, my blood splattered his shirt and turned it a brilliant red. Mr. Kessinger took me upstairs to my mom. Once the family realized I would be OK, concern shifted to that shirt. But I remember to this day that Mr. Kessinger himself could not have cared less about his shirt. He wanted to make sure I was all right.

That evening Seth approached me again. He's a teenager now. Some people might expect a little more reserve than he demonstrated. He sat next to me, leaned over, kissed my cheek and said, "Dad, I love you." Then he asked to see the scars on my forehead.

Another story had outlined another life value, another boundary, for my son. He learned that doing something for others could carry costs. There is always a price to pay — perhaps small, perhaps great.

Some 2,000 years ago, Jesus paid the ultimate price to offer lost humanity a pathway from hell to eternal life — in other words He offered us hope. Through the Word of God we find a guideline for life that is full of boundaries that give us freedom, the kind of freedom Unsión loves to tell viewers about.

CIRCUMSTANCE

lexington,
kentucky
1981

I sat in a small chair alongside Connie's bed. The room was spartan, but everything was clean and had a place. Like satellites orbiting a planet, the small metal cabinet, countertop, warming bed and bank of monitors surrounded Connie's bed.

From one of the monitors our baby's heartbeat emanated rhythmically. It was the sweet percussion of life.

"I think Billy is a fine name," I said, marveling at the machinery in the room. "Can you imagine how Leah is going to react when she meets him?"

I did not give Connie time to answer.

"Leah will help us take care of him, I'm sure," I continued, as if we had all day to chat.

"I'm sure she will," Connie said. "But don't forget that she is only 2."

"I know, but she'll be a great helper. Don't you think?"

Questions. I had asked Connie a series of them since we arrived at the hospital. Sometimes she answered, other times she did not. It all depended on the severity of her contractions. My self-appointed job was to keep her mind off the pain.

"So we're sticking with Billy, right?"

"It's a wonderful name," Connie managed to say as a contraction subsided. "Leah loves it."

"I know she does," I agreed. "So do I."

"That's understandable."

"Do you think he'll look like you or me?"

"Both of us."

"Either way is fine with me."

I leaned back in my chair and thought of the possibilities. Whose temperament would he have? Would he like football? What would he dream of being someday? Who would he look like?

"Here comes another one," Connie said, grimacing in pain. "I hate these."

I reached between the rails and grabbed her hand. It was difficult to see her suffering through the contractions, but I knew each one brought us closer to meeting Billy for the first time.

"You can do this, honey," I cheered, clasping her hand. "Hang in there. Before you know it, this will all be over."

"That's easy for you to say!"

As I forced a laugh, Connie strained as the contraction hit its apex. Tears formed in her eyes as her face contorted. When the contraction subsided she thrust her upper body back into the pile of pillows as if she were trying to disappear from the reality of her situation.

"Good job, babe," I said. "Another one down."

Connie closed her eyes and tried to relax or block out my cheer-leading. I was not sure which and was not brave enough to ask. To soothe her I reminisced about when our daughter, Leah, was born. I also made sure to tell her she looked beautiful and that I loved her.

"How bad is it when you have contractions?" I asked, returning to the safe ground of an inquiry.

Connie nodded and grimaced. Her response told me more than words could, so I dropped the subject and gently stroked her arm making sure not to bump her IV.

Billy would be our second child. The prospect of having a son to hang around with thrilled me beyond measure.

"This is one of the greatest days of my life," I said eagerly.

"Mine too, but I could do without these contractions."

Connie forced a smile as I stared at her belly, which was swathed in sheets and blankets. Doing so, I could not help but feel thankful for the gift of life I would soon hold in my arms.

"Thank You, Jesus, for my son," I prayed silently. "Give him health, joy and a future."

unexpected

As Connie's body continued its work, the labor and delivery nurse came and went. When she was with us she was extremely attentive. She looked to see how dilated Connie was, checked the heart monitors, scribbled notes onto a clipboard and adjusted the pillows. She even had a sweet disposition and soothing voice reserved only for Connie.

"Only a little while longer," she whispered. "Do you want some ice chips?"

Connie nodded.

When the nurse returned she handed Connie the cup of crushed ice and patted her arm.

"I'm going to have the doctor come in here in a few minutes," she said. "We'll be right back."

Connie poured some chips into her mouth and crunched on them. The contractions were coming faster now, and any reprieve she got from the pain was cherished.

"I can't wait to have this baby," she said.

"He'll come soon enough."

"That's easy for you to say!"

I blushed as I realized my mistake.

Just then the doctor walked in. He greeted Connie by asking her how she felt. As usual, she was upbeat and said things could not be better considering the circumstance.

As the doctor checked Connie, his voice and demeanor became serious. Though they gave me pause, I did not suspect anything was wrong.

"Mrs. McDonald," he said as he moved to Connie's bedside. "The baby is breech. If he can't get himself turned around, we're going to have to do a C-section."

Connie nodded as I strained to hear every word the doctor was saying. He seemed cool, collected and confident, so I didn't worry.

"It's nothing to be concerned about yet," continued the doctor. "But we'll see how he does here in the next hour or so. If he turns, that's great. But if he doesn't …"

Connie smiled. She did not seem too worried either. After all, babies are breech all the time. I did not like the idea of her having to go through surgery after suffering so many contractions, but we were ready to do whatever it required to meet Billy.

Despite the comfort, we both felt the following hour was tense. In between contractions we prayed that Billy would turn and that God would keep him and Connie safe.

When the doctor returned and again checked on Billy's position, he forced a smile.

"Mr. McDonald, you're going to have to step outside," he said. "We're going to have to do a C-section. As soon as we can, we'll let you back in to see your son."

painful

I leaned over and kissed Connie on the forehead as other medical personnel came into the room. We prayed a quick prayer and she said, "I love you," before I headed for the door.

"I love you too," I said. "Billy will be here soon."

I walked toward the door as the doctors and nurses turned their attention to Connie. With the precision and efficiency of a well-oiled machine, the medical team prepped for the operation. I was determined not to leave, so I stopped short of the door and hid in the shadows of the portico. The doctors and nurses were so busy that none of them noticed me.

As the doctors and nurses became consumed with the procedure, I strained to get a glimpse of my son. I wanted to see Billy the moment they pulled him from the womb. As the team worked, I could only imagine what Billy looked like. Seconds later the doctor extracted Billy from Connie's womb, but I did not get a good look at him. Even so, my excitement swelled.

But it was short-lived. I heard the doctor mutter some medical jargon I could not understand. Then I got a long glimpse of Billy. He looked like he was dead. His tiny body and head were completely blue — as if he had suffocated.

More medical terminology flowed from the doctor's mouth as the nurses scrambled to care for Billy. Their frenzied pace made me feel sick, and I wanted to rush into the room and try to solve all Billy's problems.

I was a young pastor at the time, believing God for everything — including the health of my baby boy. But in an instant my world was being rocked to its core. I stumbled into the hallway having seen more than I could handle. Tears brimmed in my eyes.

Suddenly time did not matter, and I felt very lonely. Several minutes later the doctor emerged from the room. His compassionate face conveyed the mood brewing inside me.

"Mr. McDonald," he said gravely. "I'm afraid I have some bad news."

I nodded.

"Your baby is microcephalic."

"I've never even heard of that; what does it mean?"

The doctor's shoulders slumped as he spoke. "Being microcephalic means your son's brain has not grown the way it should have. He has a small brain."

"So, how do we correct that?"

"We can't," the doctor said. "Your son is going to die. I'm so sorry."

As the words left the doctor's mouth, I felt as if I was a wax man melting onto a hot plate.

"It would be best if you tell your wife," continued the doctor. "She needs to hear this from you rather than us."

comforted

I nodded again and tried — with little success — to catch my breath. The hall seemed to be spinning as I walked aimlessly down it. Suddenly my legs felt heavy as if I was trudging through waist-deep cement.

For a moment I wanted to express my displeasure to God by pointing my finger at Him and asking why He would let my son suffer. But as I prepared to make my case, another overwhelming feeling invaded me. For reasons I could not understand, I felt an urgent need to praise and thank God.

"Thank You, Lord," I cried with arms raised toward heaven. "Thank You, Jesus. You have a plan and a purpose for Billy's life. I give him to You, Lord."

An hour later I made my way to Connie's room. She seemed peaceful and content, though I knew she knew something was wrong. I leaned over and bowed my head. She took my head in her hands.

"Billy's not going to live," I sobbed.

Connie pulled me close as if she knew beforehand exactly what I was going to say.

"It's all going to be OK, Billy," she said softly. "Don't worry."

But I did. For several days I wrestled with a lack of hope that was robbing me, until I realized that God wanted me to put every ounce of hope I had in Him. When I finally did, amazing things began to happen.

I wanted to put a good front up for Connie and everyone else, but truth be told I was scared and very worried. The blow we had been dealt had me searching for a bunker to get some respite. I found such a place in my journal.

July 17, 1981

Last night I stayed the night with Connie. I could not have left her side if I had to. Everyone has been so nice and kind. I thought Thursday was hard, but today Connie was able to hold Billy. As I stood there and looked upon my son in his mother's arms my heart was broken all over again, but this time into a million pieces. I have never felt pain like this before. I am falling in love with my son and my wife all over again.

I noticed today that I am all mixed up and confused. The only thing that matters right now is Billy, Leah and Connie — and, of course, my relationship to God. But my religiosity doesn't matter much at this moment though God as my Father means everything to me.

I showed Leah a picture of Billy and told her that this was her baby brother. She smiled and called him Billy Boy. She can't understand why Daddy is crying.

Little Baby,
Rest in Mommy's Arms
Daddy Loves You So
And Wants to Keep You
From all Harm

At Unsión
we believe he who tells the story shapes the culture

He who tells the story shapes the culture. We live and die by that saying at Unsión.

One playwright described the storytelling art as not a mirror held up to society, but a hammer by which to shape it. Theater, film, television and books — they shape our culture.

The God-serving storyteller will change the world one soul at a time by proclaiming Kingdom truths and values in a manner that gives full life to a living message. At Unsión we do that by fulfilling four requirements: As believers we know our stories, we share our stories with the world at large, we tell other people's stories, and we help other followers of Christ tell their stories to the widest audience possible.

It is my contention that we have to know why we are here, what we are about, and where we are going in life and in eternity. That is the story of the Bible lived out in each of us. As we tell that story we shape our world.

There used to be days when I was scared to death of Jehovah's Witnesses. On the surface, they seemed so secure in their religious arguments. I felt like my biblical responses were ineffective and I would be viewed as the village idiot. But over the years I discovered a wonderful response to Jehovah's Witnesses: my story.

Now when a Jehovah's Witness engages me in conversation I do not hesitate to tell him stories of my life and faith. It is not a complicated or intimidating thing to do. In sharing my story, I am exercising an opportunity — maybe my only opportunity — to show someone else Jesus.

As a follower of Christ, when we tell the story of our changed lives and our love for God, we put into use the greatest weapon in our arsenal against any other worldview or doctrine.

Over the years one thing I have observed about people is they are rarely convinced by an argument; instead, they are usually convinced to change their minds by who we are and how God has transformed us.

That is one reason Unsión loves to tell stories of faith. When we share what God is doing in other people's lives on television, we harmonize with the work of His Spirit. Whether that is through sharing the life lessons found in Scripture, or the life testimonies of great men and women of God today, there are a host of powerful stories to be told.

I follow the same philosophy when I preach. Though my kids sometimes squirm when I share their stories, I love doing so.

For instance, I often tell of when Leah was 5 years old. She had locked herself in the bathroom. Connie became concerned after a while, so she listened at the door. She heard Leah praying. When the door opened, Connie said, "Leah, what were you doing in there?"

"I was getting saved," Leah told her.

"You mean you prayed to receive Jesus as your Lord and Savior?" Connie asked proudly.

"Yeah, that's what I just did."

Over the years we've used that story again and again to point people of all ages to Jesus. Also, in telling Leah's story, the event has been solidified in her own mind. I think if you asked Leah today when she gave her heart to Jesus she would say in the bathroom on Clay Street at the age of 5.

Another way to use story to shape culture is to empower people to share their stories with as many people as possible.

One of the best ways to do that is to support the artistic work of people who are telling our story of faith through projects that reach a wide range of audiences.

I regularly implore people to get behind producers of not just Christian films, but projects that communicate Kingdom values. Write to local stations that air good TV programs. Be a widely heard voice for godly standards in all the media, whether you see those standards promoted in film, music or in a powerful book. Stand with storytellers who faithfully exercise their gift and make a difference. If someone makes a great movie that exalts Jesus, pay eight bucks and see it.

As Christ followers and broadcasters we realize we are conduits of the greatest story ever told. Because of it we are committed to following the example of the greatest marketplace storyteller who ever existed — Jesus himself.

Think of Christ's parables. They were popular. Through them He drew great crowds. People came and experienced life with Him, whether through a meal or a story. Jesus ministered to the masses utilizing a positive message as good entertainment with a spiritual truth embedded in the story.

Our show *Cocinemos*, or *Cooking Together*, is hosted by a former Miss Ecuador. She is just a mom cooking a great meal for her children. She does not preach; she teaches people how to cook. But she tells the story of cooking in such a way the Christian story is always embedded. When she is interviewed she always refers to her faith. Her strength and purpose are from God. Her show is having an impact in prisons where televisions have been installed so women can learn how to cook.

That is just one example of how Unsión creates programming that allows us to slowly introduce viewers to a Christian lifestyle and eventually to Christ. It's an interactive ministry that brings viewer response by phone, snail mail, e-mail and to our Web site. As I mentioned earlier, so far more than 45,000 viewers have made decisions to follow Christ.

That proves to me that he who tells the story shapes the culture.

EXPECTED

For the next two weeks Billy became a part of our lives. We took turns spending our days and evenings at the hospital doing whatever the doctors would let us do to connect with Billy. Though his prognosis was grim, an undeniable bond formed. All of us were able to look past the tubes and wires and innocently believe for a miracle.

When Leah saw her baby brother she called him Billy Boy. The name stuck, and with no regard for Billy Boy's bleak prognosis we talked of his future and what his life would be like when God healed him.

Some people would say we were being naïve, but when you have nowhere to turn but your faith, you have to believe for the best no matter what. For some people that may take awhile to achieve, but it is the best way to live.

After I conquered my initial doubts I wanted nothing more than to take our baby home and watch him grow into a healthy boy. After all, our desires were not too much for God to handle. He could heal Billy Boy in an instant if He chose to do so. Since that was a possibility, we believed it would happen.

When Billy was stable enough the doctors allowed him to go home. His prognosis was still bleak, but the move gave all of us a measure of hope that had been eluding us, and we were grateful for that.

devastated

As I walked in the door the night of my 28th birthday, Connie stood in the living room waiting for me. In her arms she held Billy. I noticed immediately her face was tear-streaked. My heart sank.

"Billy just died," she said looking down at him. "He's with the Lord now, Bill."

My body shuddered, and the tears came easily. Of course, I was sad because Billy died, but what broke my heart were the thoughts of what would have been for Billy.

I would never know if he would grow up to look like me or if he would ever preach a sermon or be a star quarterback. I would never get to meet the girl of his dreams or stand over his shoulder while he did his homework. I would never know what it would be like to go fishing with him or stay up late watching a movie with him.

Not knowing what could have been for Billy hurt the most. I just wanted to know what God had in store for him. But as the weeks turned to months and the months to years, I realized I would never know, in this life, what would have been for Billy.

In time our hearts slowly healed. Looking back now, I can honestly say my faith never wavered. Even though things did not turn out the way I hoped they would, I never once regretted hoping God would heal Billy.

After all, by leaving Billy's life in God's hands I was allowing God to not only walk with me, but also guide me through some of the saddest days of my life. In those days I learned there is no greater Comforter than God.

A year later Connie talked openly about her desire to continue expanding our family. We discussed our options with her doctors, and all of them were in agreement that Billy's condition was an anomaly.

Two years after that meeting Connie got pregnant again. Though the doctors were confident we would not have another baby who was microcephalic, they kept close tabs on Connie and the baby.

Each ultrasound confirmed Connie and the baby were doing fine. But during Connie's five-month checkup the nurse doing the ultrasound guessed out loud that the baby girl Connie was carrying must be 3 months old.

"Why do you say 3 months?" Connie inquired suspiciously.

"You can see by the circumference of her head," the nurse said. "She is about 3 months."

Four months later, Katherine Lee was born — like Billy, she was microcephalic. On Christmas night two months after her birth, Katie died.

The only thing that gave us comfort was that she was in heaven with Billy Boy.

At Unsión
we believe God is greater than the odds against us

Television is one of the best and most efficient ways to convey Christ's message of love and hope. Studies show that prior to 1950, 49 percent of Americans attended a house of worship on a weekly basis. Pulpits across the United States formed a united front of ethical and spiritual orientation, and the church held the reins of mass communication via their congregations. In many ways the church was America's storyteller and established itself as a major voice in the marketplace, thus shaping the culture.

Today, it is not a stretch to say the church has lost its voice in the marketplace. This is partly due to television — a technology that gained its footing in the 1950s and has never looked back. Shortly after its introduction to the mainstream market, television began to gather a large audience. Within just a few months there were as many people watching television as were gathering in houses of worship.

Not surprisingly church attendance has diminished in the decades since television entered our living rooms. Today, the average American watches three and a half hours of television per day, but spends only an average of three and a half minutes per day in church.

Since our pulpits have lost much of their influence in today's culture, a consistent injection of a strong, Christian worldview into culture is absent. In its place are competing philosophies that push moral mores on every level imaginable. Television has proven to be one of the greatest tools for advancing such worldviews. Why wouldn't it? After all, it is the storyteller of our day.

It would be difficult to deny that television affects our values, attitudes and worldview. Over time, the three and a half hours of daily television the average American digests will either reinforce or corrode his or her values.

There is a war underway! It's the kind of war that will shape our values, our culture and, inevitably, our future. Because the storytellers have the leverage in this battle, followers of Christ must continue to fight for a right to tell the greatest story ever told.

A while back, Spanish-language media giant Univision Communications Inc. was looking at putting itself up for sale, according to a report in The New York Times. The sale would likely draw the biggest names in the media, and it was estimated that Univision was worth about $10 billion at the time.

There are many ways to evaluate the influential power of Univision, but, for the sake of simplicity, consider the following. During prime time, Univision has a viewing audience of 5 million viewers, as compared to other major broadcasters such as ABC, CBS, and NBC that can have as many as 19 million viewers each during the same time frame.

Simply stated, Univision is probably — at best — a quarter of the strength of any of the big three networks in the United States. Even so, media powerbrokers saw a good deal when they ran the numbers. It would cost approximately $2,000 to reach each of Univision's 5 million viewers.

Certainly not chump change, but still a very good deal. I can say that with a straight face because I know that the people telling the stories are influencing culture. They know that by having our undivided attention for three and a half hours a day they can influence every major area of our lives: our voting habits, what we eat, what products we consume, whom or what we will worship, and even expand our views on sexual orientation.

The Church has only two options, as far as I can see.

First, we can allow ourselves the option of taking no action and allow the powerbrokers to purchase the position of culture's storyteller while Christ's followers embrace an "ark" mentality — saving only our own and remaining comfortable.

Or we can choose to engage culture by introducing positive change through powerful storytelling on television. It's not too late. If we are willing to pay the price, we can become serious players in the battle for the heart and soul of Hispanic viewers throughout the world.

CALLED

uisville,
entucky
1987

The world map before me was colorful and large. It took up an entire wall in our church's chapel and was so massive I could not help but dream about foreign lands.

"Lord, protect the people of France and Mali," I prayed one morning out loud in the cavernous chapel. "Meet their needs. Provide miracles for them so that they may know You. Send missionaries who will spread Your gospel…"

Before I knew it, praying for other countries was becoming a habit. At the time, I had no desire to be a missionary. I just knew that praying and listening to the prompting of the Holy Spirit was crucial to my faith walk. As a staff member at Evangel Tabernacle [now Evangel World Prayer Center] in Louisville, Kentucky, I spent a portion of each morning in prayer.

Like most people, I had certain things I would pray for: those who had yet to commit their lives to Christ, the safety of missionaries, the effectiveness of our ministries, and for my family and friends.

Inevitably, I would conclude my prayer time by praying for countries around the world. I chose countries to pray for at random but always prayed for Ecuador. I would lay my hands on the postage-stamp-sized country wedged between Colombia, Peru and the Pacific Ocean. Though I knew little about Ecuador and was not even sure if I was pronouncing its name correctly, I could not escape my desire to pray for it daily.

"*Lord of the Harvest, send laborers into Your harvest field,*" I would pray, paraphrasing Luke 10:2. "Prepare the hearts of people all over the world. Send brave and willing missionaries to Ecuador so others might know You."

I did not know any Ecuadorians, and, to be honest, I had no interest in meeting anyone from Ecuador. I was sure Spanish was spoken in Ecuador, but the only Spanish words I was comfortable throwing around were taco, enchilada and burrito.

Despite my limited knowledge of the country, I was drawn to it each morning. As time passed, my prayers for Ecuador moved from general needs to more specific ones.

"Lord, send someone to Ecuador," I prayed one morning. "Prepare his or her heart and give him or her the courage to go."

I began to find myself thinking about the tiny country throughout the day. One morning I awoke feeling frustrated about why I was continually drawn to Ecuador.

Did God want me to rally our church to support missions in the country?

Did He want me to continue to only pray that He would send someone there as a missionary?

Did He want me to support a ministry there financially?

What change in my life or ministry did He want me to make?

For weeks the questions came faster than the answers. Ecuador was not only on my mind; it was invading my heart.

focused

When Leah was 3 years old and wanted to get my attention, she would grab both of my ears and pull her face to mine until we were touching noses. Then she would look into my eyes and say, "I'm a talk'n to you!"

I decided to take the same approach with God regarding Ecuador. I wanted to be bold and throw myself at His mercy and tell Him exactly how I was feeling so that I could find out why He was burdening me with thoughts of Ecuador.

"Lord, what is it about Ecuador?" I asked as I knelt down in the chapel and began my morning ritual. The only difference this day was that I was a bit more animated as I prayed. "Please, show me what You need from me regarding Ecuador. What do You want from me?"

They were innocent enough questions, but the answers I felt I received from God took me by surprise. Throughout my life I believe God has spoken to me. Not in an audible way, but through visions and thoughts that are so powerful, so right and so true I believe they can only come from God.

"I want you to answer your own prayer," is what I would later tell people God said to me that morning.

When I pulled myself up off the floor I was sure of only one thing — God wanted Connie and me to go to Ecuador as missionaries.

I was so sure of the calling that I immediately drove back to our home, which was three minutes from the church, to share my good news with Connie. Why wouldn't I? She was the one I loved the most, and she would be the one who had to move with me to fulfill the vision I had received from God. Grinning from ear to ear, I bounded through our front door and into the entryway.

"Connie!" I yelled. "Where are you?"

Connie emerged from the kitchen with a coffee cup in hand. She looked shocked to see me, and I dashed toward her with my arms open wide and a smile filling my face.

"Bill, are you OK?"

"I just heard from the Lord," I said. "You aren't going to believe what I'm going to tell you."

After we hugged, Connie set her coffee mug on the counter and stepped back from me as if I were a crazy man.

"Well, what'd He say?" she asked, getting to the point.

"You won't believe this." Since she probably would not have, I wanted to prepare her. I grabbed her coffee then led her to the kitchen table where we sat down. "The Lord called me, I mean us, to be missionaries to Ecuador."

I expected Connie to say she had a similar conversation with God just moments ago. But she did not. I expected her to say she would follow me to the ends of the earth. But she did not. I expected her to say Ecuador had been on her heart too. But she did not.

Instead she weighed my words and sipped her coffee. The silence was unbearable, but I patiently waited for her to speak.

"And who is going to be your wife in Ecuador?" she asked flatly.

"My wife?"

"Yeah, who is going to be your wife in Ecuador?"

"You, of course."

"I'm not going to Ecuador."

"But honey, we've been called."

Connie shook her head. "You think you've been called, but God hasn't called me."

"Well, I know that. I mean, He called me; I'm sure He'll call you."

"When and if He does, I'll let you know."

unmoved

Connie's unwillingness to jump on my bandwagon left me stumped. I went back to the church a bit deflated but was sure I had heard from God. When Connie had asked me who my wife would be in Ecuador the tone of her voice was deadly serious. Though God had been bombarding me with thoughts of Ecuador, it was not even on her radar.

Why would it be?

Our daughter, Leah, attended a wonderful school, we were living in Louisville near both sets of our parents, and we were on staff at our home church, which had a vibrant and growing congregation. Life was very good. There was no sense in stirring things up just so I could settle my restless soul.

In many ways Connie's response was exactly what I expected. In other ways, it was far from what I wanted to hear. But one thing I have learned is that when God gives us a big calling He gives us a surplus of grace and even more determination. I believe He requires us to dispense and wield such things with care.

If Connie did not feel called by God to go to Ecuador, what business did I have dragging her down there?

God still needed to work on her heart if I had heard Him correctly, or He needed to change my mind if I was wrong. Either way, I had to turn the situation over to Him, which I did.

As I drove back to work, instead of thinking of ways to convince Connie that we needed to go to Ecuador I prayed that if we were really to be missionaries, God must make it clear to her too. I figured if God had really called me to be a missionary then He'd call her too.

The days turned into weeks, and Connie did not say a word about Ecuador and neither did I. Even so, my desire to go to Ecuador did not wane; in fact it increased. But one weekend while traveling everything changed.

"Bill, I have a surprise for you," Connie said, as she handed me a package.

"What is it?"

"Well, open it and you'll find out."

Carefully I opened the little package in my hands. Inside of it was a small brass globe and attached to it was a small handwritten note, "I will go anywhere in the world with you."

"Are you sure?"

Connie nodded. We embraced. Once again, God had proven faithful. But just because we were called to go to Ecuador and were willing to go did not mean that things would be easy.

In fact we were just about to learn that doing something out of the ordinary for God could be fraught with challenges. And ours were only just beginning.

At Unsión
we believe we are a network of character

One of Unsión's main goals is to be an influential voice to Hispanic viewers around the world. Because of our unique business/ministry model, we can compete in the general market and yet present the message of Christ without compromise.

At Unsión we do not believe the sacred and the secular are mutually exclusive. In other words, we have stepped into the secular world to tell a sacred story.

In broadcasting fun-to-watch family-values programming, we creatively attempt to engage our viewers' minds with thoughts that challenge their worldview and value systems. Unsión's broadcast day is much like that of a secular network's, with the exception that every 30 minutes we show 30-second spots that speak directly to the spiritual condition of our viewers.

Being upfront about our beliefs demonstrates to viewers Jesus, the One who can transform today's family. We have grown with a clear vision in mind: To promote and sow Christian values in our society through providing entertainment, information and education of the highest moral, ethical and entertainment standards.

We have made the decision, before God and society, to show ourselves transparent. We will not contradict our biblical philosophy with our administrative and commercial actions.

Unsión does not entertain business associations with companies that sell services or products that jeopardize our viewers' health and well-being. Instead, we aggressively recruit partnerships with those who hold to our high standards.

We match our media with our message to shape the culture of the Hispanic world. The hungry are fed, lives are changed, and we are anchored when serving as a standard for a new generation who will see Unsión as their network.

We aim to be a network with a message! The kind of message that can transform people's lives and lead them to an eternity with Jesus.

Since Unsión was founded, we have discovered that to accomplish our goals we must continually tap our wells of creativity. Without a doubt, doing so is crucial in getting viewers to change the channel on their viewing habits.

CONSEQUENCE

The table was set. We put out our fine china and crystal. We had serving platters brimming with turkey, stuffing, potatoes, sweet yams, gravy and rolls on our dining room table.

In the living room a fully decorated tree complete with tinsel, colorful lights and presents underneath awaited us. Bing Crosby's "White Christmas" emanated from somewhere in the back of the house. The intoxicating aroma of turkey and sugar cookies hung in the air. My in-laws, Dick and Lee Givan, had come to have Christmas with us. It promised to be a day of joy, sharing and peace.

Ever since Connie had given me the brass globe, we had prayed and thought about the best time to tell our parents we were going to be missionaries. We settled on Christmas Day for her parents.

"I can hardly wait to tell them," I told Connie that Christmas morning. "We're following God's calling on our lives. I'm sure they'll support that."

"Of course they will," Connie affirmed. "How could they not be happy for us?"

We gathered around the dining room table, prayed and then dug into the feast before us. The clinking of dishes and silverware competed with the chatter of a family glad to be together on such a wonderful day. As we ate, Connie and I were bubbling with excitement as we looked for the perfect moment to make our announcement.

As each minute passed, both of us were finding it hard not to blurt out our plans to go to the mission field. Knowing our timing had to be right, we let the tension and excitement of the moment build. Not wanting to shock everyone with the news, we looked for the perfect spot during the course of conversation to spring our big surprise.

After Leah excused herself to the living room to eyeball all the gifts and speculate what she was getting for Christmas, Connie gave me a nod that the moment we were looking for was upon us.

"We have some exciting news," I began as I reached over and held Connie's hand. I could only imagine what her parents were thinking. They probably thought we were going to say Connie was pregnant or I got a promotion or we were going to buy a new house.

I let my words hang in the air just a bit to ramp up the drama of what I was going to tell them.

"A few months ago, after much prayer and discussion," I continued, "Connie and I believe God called us to the mission field."

"The mission field?" asked my mother-in-law.

Connie nodded.

"We're moving to Ecuador," I said, "to plant churches."

"Ecuador?" her mother asked.

"I went there during World War II, and there isn't anything down there except for seafood," Dick said, with eyebrows raised — whether in concern or disbelief, I wasn't sure.

"It's not too far from here," I said.

"Is it safe there?" Lee asked.

By the tone of their voices and their looks of dismay, I quickly realized our big news was not going to be as celebrated as we thought. Instead, it seemed as if we had just punched each of them in the stomach and left them gasping for air.

"Of course it is," Connie said.

"I saw that place in *National Geographic*, Bill," Lee said. "If you need adventure, go to the jungles in Africa for a few weeks, but don't drag our little girl down to South America for the rest of her life."

I swallowed hard. Connie gripped my hand. Our little announcement had suddenly zapped any Christmas cheer in the house. We thought we were giving her parents a gift; it was anything but that.

reevaluate

Where we saw opportunity, they saw tragedy. That's the nature of change sometimes.

Suddenly, all the romantic notions we had held of becoming missionaries evaporated like steam coming off a street.

"I can't argue with God," I said. "Connie and I truly believe He called us to Ecuador. We're looking at it as an opportunity of a lifetime."

The rest of the day was somewhat of a letdown for all of us. Connie's parents were sad that their daughter and granddaughter were moving away. We were disappointed they weren't as excited as we had hoped they would be.

That night as we tried to sleep, Connie and I were both deflated. The day had spun out of control. Her parents wanted us near them and had imagined growing old having their granddaughter nearby. I couldn't blame them for having strong feelings against our move.

But sometimes God calls us to do things that will disrupt our lives and those of the ones we love. Fulfilling God's vision for our lives sometimes requires stepping out of our comfort zones. Change is hard, but Connie and I knew for certain God had called us to Ecuador.

I was also quickly realizing that becoming a missionary was a risky and costly endeavor. We were not only forfeiting our position at the church, we were leaving behind our home, families, friends and way of life. Nothing would ever be the same again.

Part of me wanted to second-guess myself, but the draw on my soul to step outside my comfort zone and do something big for God was stronger than ever. There was no turning back. We were going to Ecuador. If for no other reason than to be obedient to the vision God had given us.

"It's all going to work out," I whispered to Connie. "I promise you that."

"I know it will," said Connie as she moved closer to me. "But it doesn't make leaving any easier."

If we thought dealing with family issues was tough, what awaited us in Ecuador was going to be grueling at worst and heart wrenching at the very least.

But at that moment we had no idea.

At Unsión
we believe creativity is paramount

The pornography industry is the most lucrative media juggernaut today. Billions of dollars pour in to producers of sexually explicit movies, and their production costs are next to nothing compared to legitimate filmmaking.

Tragically, pornography's hedonistic themes are moving in diluted form into mainstream television and film. Series like Sex and the City, Nip Tuck and Desperate Housewives, and film franchises like American Pie portray a sexual free-for-all and draw in lucrative percentages of the viewing market.

What is happening here? Why such popularity for the most debasing of themes? It's really quite simple. Such material is falsely presented as "entertainment" with the claim of no harm done. The story lines within these products rarely hint at the emotional and spiritual devastation of sexual promiscuity. There might be the occasional plotline of a jilted lover or jealous spouse, but even then the focus of the film or episode remains the physical passion portrayed.

And film is not the only culprit. Increasingly, the video game industry seeks to lure players into virtual environments where they can act out their most depraved fantasies with no consequences. Players deal out death, destruction, profanity and immorality in a world of ever-more-detailed pixels and sound effects.

Many other young people across this country have never learned respect for human life because they know of no larger story or narrative or vision to take them beyond the level of self-absorption and self-indulgence. For too many children and teens, the story lines they envision are very limited, and the portrayed purpose of existence does not go beyond immediate thrills, shows of bravado and casual sex.

But there are few entertainment entities offered from the other end of the moral spectrum. Many of the secular classics of yesteryear find less and less airtime. And the great majority of Christian media offerings, to this point, have not carried the kind of message needed to even begin attracting this generation's attention.

Say "Christian movie," for example, to most followers of Christ and they will find it difficult if not impossible to keep from thinking of words like "boring," "naïve," "clichéd," or even "awful." "Christian television" too readily brings to mind "used car salesmen" caricatures of televangelists or deadly earnest and somber televised sermons.

Most Christians forget how dramatic the Bible is and the awesome spectrum of life experience portrayed in its pages. God's Word pulls no punches in describing life and death and passion and adventure. The difference is, God's Word always makes a clear connection between actions and reactions, between decisions and consequences. And God's Word always makes good attractive, while warning against evil.

Unsión is committed to following that biblical model. We do not do Christian television per se, but we do produce values-based television that entertains the entire family and teaches clear lessons about life. We have on the drawing board a soap opera that will unapologetically deal with all the "bad" themes of life. The difference is that episodes of our soap opera will show the consequences and will point viewers toward right choices.

The church has what it takes to become competitive on the entertainment world scene. The key is creativity. If Christians possess the Spirit of the Creator God, then Christians should be the most creative people on the planet. And there are certainly examples to bear this out.

J.R.R. Tolkien's *Lord of the Rings* trilogy, when adapted to film, garnered multiple Oscars and a worldwide audience. Tolkien, a committed Christian, creatively developed a rich mythic Middle Earth that used fictional creatures to paint a panoramic vision of war between good and evil. The *Chronicles of Narnia* books of C.S. Lewis, Tolkien's contemporary, have moved to the big screen to great acclaim.

When creativity is a production's clear strength, that production will draw an audience from across social, economic and even religious lines.

The spark separating a work of creative genius from another run-of-the-mill narrative lights a fire of curiosity in the viewer and invites him or her to leave behind the challenges of life for a few minutes or hours. And in that window of rest and intrigue, the heart and mind can be sparked with a desire to seek out better things, even eternal things.

VERSITY

cuenca,
ecuador

Several times a month the missionary forded swollen rivers, trudged through miles of muddy trails, endured unbearable heat and humidity, and fought off swarms of mosquitoes. His goal was simple. He wanted to bring the gospel to a remote village deep in the rain forest.

But he had a problem, a very big problem. Each time he traveled to the village, his offering of friendship was rejected by the village chief and elders. They wanted nothing to do with him.

He was determined — God had called him, he said, to reach that village for Christ. Because of it, he continued his treks out to the village on a regular basis. And each time he arrived, the village chief and his elders shunned him.

As the months wore on, the missionary grew frustrated and decided he would give the village leaders one more chance to accept his offer of friendship. But once again he was rebuffed.

So discouraged was the missionary that he decided to give up and never return to the village. As he dejectedly walked out of the village he used the theme of Jesus' words to defend his decision, "I'll shake the dust of this place off my feet."

But just as those words rolled off his tongue, he said, the Lord pointed out to him that the only thing on his boots was mud.

Looking down at his muddy boots, a renewed determination to reach the village with the gospel overcame him. He decided he would continue to trek back to the village for as long as it took for at least one person from the village to commit his or her life to Christ. After many more months, and at least as many more rejections, a man came to Christ. Today, there is a church in the village.

determined

Within weeks of moving to Cuenca, I felt like the aforementioned missionary. In every way, I wanted to shake the dust of Cuenca — even Ecuador — off my feet and go back to the safe life we had in Kentucky.

Dark, menacing clouds hung low over Cuenca, making the air frigid, thin and unforgiving. Like many places during winter, everything in Cuenca felt grey, cold and lifeless — including myself.

In an attempt to get acquainted with the city and acclimated to the culture, Connie and I spent many hours driving and walking through Cuenca getting a sense of our new community. We immediately fell in love with the cobblestone streets, colonial architecture, distinctive food and way of life. But what captivated us were the people. They were warm, kind and welcoming. But we sensed very quickly that, though the people might have liked us on a personal level, many of them had no desire to talk about Jesus. That reality left me feeling depressed.

To add to that feeling were the holidays that loomed like a sad reminder. For the first time in our married lives, Connie and I were going to celebrate Thanksgiving and Christmas without our families.

I could not deny that the excitement that had carried me through our itineration had escaped me. Suddenly, all my idealism concerning missions was swept out the door. In its place loomed the reality that reaching people for Jesus Christ in a foreign city that was not eager to embrace our message was going to be challenging.

"Maybe we should have moved here in the spring," I told Connie as we sat in our tiny home on a cold and drizzly day. "Coming here during the holiday season was probably not the best idea."

Connie shrugged. "What're we going to do?" she asked. Not waiting for an answer, she insisted, "We're here, so there's no need to wish for something else."

"I know, I know," I said. "This just isn't what I expected."

"Well, what'd you expect?"

I shook my head. Before coming to the mission field I was optimistic to the point that I thought everything would be much easier than it actually was. That's the curse and blessing of being a person motivated by God-given dreams and visions.

"I really don't know. I just thought things would be smoother, I guess."

Weeks later, on Christmas Day, Connie, Leah and I sat in the living room reading letters and cards sent from our family and friends back in Kentucky.

"How good would some turkey, potatoes and gravy be right now?" I asked Connie with tears forming in my eyes. "Just to sit at the table with our families for 10 minutes — I'd give anything to be back home."

Connie's eyes told me she was missing her mom and dad and the Christmas traditions she had grown up with as much as I missed my parents and the customs I had come to love.

"In my mind everything was going to be different," I confessed. "I thought it would be easier to share the gospel than it is. I thought —"

"It's OK," Connie said. "This is where we're supposed to be. It'll work out. It always does."

I nodded and wanted to believe her, but my mind kept dredging up all the obstacles and hardships we had already faced. Then my thoughts would shift into overdrive and drum up worst-case scenarios.

"Things will get better," Connie said, her voice cracking with emotion. Though she wanted to be strong for Leah and me, the strain was too much, and she could not help but release some of her frustration and emotion. "They've got to get better, right?"

We both began crying. Christmas, Ecuador, our ministry nor anything about our lives was shaping up the way we expected. Loneliness seemed a constant companion, and I could not help but regret my resolve to get to Ecuador as soon as we could. Strangely, it was during this time that God was able to teach me some of life's most valuable lessons.

The first being that even though we have a calling from God on our lives that does not mean things are going to be easy.

If I were a doctor I would have diagnosed us with culture shock. Though we were yearning for a panacea to heal us, the only prescription I know of for culture shock is a complicated thing called time. Time can help heal us, but it can also feel like a cruel eternity.

Those lean months of ministry also taught me that the only way I could fail as a missionary was to quit. If I wanted God to do big things, I was going to have to take some big risks.

These realizations would take me on some of the wildest adventures I could handle, including planting churches and founding the Unsión Television.

As the new year began in Cuenca we began to settle into our lives and on the fact that life and ministry in a foreign land were not always going to be easy.

At Unsión
we believe content is king

As a boy growing up in Louisville, I had two options on television — Channel 3 and 11. That is almost laughable today. But back then I did not know differently. Turn on most televisions today and you will find a bevy of channels from which to choose, thanks to cable and satellite operators.

There is a saying in television that speaks to our present-day entertainment indulgence: "Content is king!"

Whenever I hear that, I have to agree, but in the back of my mind I cannot help but say, "It's only king because creativity is queen."

Don't believe me? Take a look at networks such as Fox, MTV and CNN. All three took big bites out of the three major networks' (ABC, NBC and CBS) viewership by offering loads of fresh and creative content. In many ways, Fox, MTV and CNN revolutionized the television industry by creating a demand for more and more channels stuffed with creative content.

We are storytelling creatures who devour stories (both true and fictional) as if they were hotcakes at the International House of Pancakes. We just cannot seem to get enough. Because of this insatiable desire and the television industry's willingness to cater to our needs, we have opened ourselves up to whatever they will feed us.

The entertainment industry has been successful in molding young minds because it supplies them with stories, dramas and images. If moral educators are to be successful in helping children to resist the attractions of media's less-desirable elements, they need to pay more attention to the role of imagination in moral growth.

It's important to provide youngsters with codes of conduct. It's important to help them develop good habits. But it's equally important to feed their imaginations with moral stories. Just as the imagination and the passions can be enlisted on the side of vice, so also, and with a little more effort, they can be enlisted on the side of virtue.

I believe a proper moral education involves three things: training of the reason, training of the will, and training of the imagination. We used to understand this in America, and we used to understand how to cultivate character: by enforcing discipline, creating a positive moral culture in the school, presenting youngsters with high ideals and good examples, and by motivating them with powerful stories.

Somewhere along the way we forgot how to do this. We stopped telling the kinds of stories that could provide a meaningful vision of life; we ridiculed the whole idea of habit formation. We experimented, instead, with various supposed shortcuts, such as values clarification and decision-making.

Powerful individuals, institutions, organizations and movements want to shape our society's belief system, shape what your kids will believe, whom they will serve and what they will buy. These entities are culture brokers. Your future is on the auction block, and guess who is bidding?

Christ's followers must fight fire with fire. It's up to us to provide the next generation with stories, images and memories that will help them make sense out of their lives, resist the nihilism of popular culture, and at the same time inspire them to do the right thing.

OBEDIENT

cuenca,
ecuador
1989

I looked at the fledgling congregation before me. Missionaries Juan Angel and Edith Castro and their two children, Karen and Daniel, plus another family Juan had invited to our church sat with Connie and Leah. In all there were 11 of us. This fact did not deter me. In fact, it emboldened me.

"This church needs to be a missionary church," I proclaimed from my makeshift pulpit. "It needs to be a church that is constantly saying: Who can we help? Who can we tell about the Lord?"

The fledgling congregation nodded in agreement.

When I came to Ecuador, I had a church planting strategy that was straightforward and simple: Reach people with the gospel by serving them without hesitation. Though I did not hesitate to share my views, and my audience was behind me 100 percent, I would soon discover that growing a church in Ecuador, let alone planting another one, was easier said than done.

Ecuador is about the size of Nevada. Cuenca is in the southern part of the country, 9,000 feet above sea level and nestled in the Andes Mountains. During the Inca Empire, Cuenca was at the heart of that storied civilization. Though the city of 500,000 residents has an illustrious past, I learned that an evangelical presence was less than vigorous and many residents were fiercely resistant to the gospel.

Even so, our goal was to share our faith, disciple believers and plant churches. But to do any of those things, I needed some committed Christian nationals.

"Lord, send me a man or woman that You can use to plant a daughter church," I prayed regularly. "I need someone who wants to be a minister and a missionary."

As I prayed, I sensed God wanted me to plant a daughter church in Cumbe, a community 30 minutes south of Cuenca. As I investigated Cumbe, I discovered there was not one evangelical church there — in my estimation that made it a perfect place to plant one.

disciple

But the question still remained: Who would go? After all, our burgeoning congregation needed me. Plus, establishing an indigenous church is much easier when the leadership team is made up of nationals.

The answer to my prayers came in the person of an eager young man named Juan Vincent.

On a Sunday morning, Juan, whom I had led to Christ a few months earlier, bounded into church as he did every week. Juan had a quick smile and was extremely enthusiastic about sharing his faith. He had also made fast work becoming an integral part of our congregation by serving and embracing any leadership opportunity that came his way.

Though he was a model congregant, I was unaware of his ambitions until he came into church wearing a tie. Ties, in and of themselves, are not unusual in Ecuador. But they do stand out in a church — especially on people who are not pastors.

As I spoke that morning my eyes were drawn to Juan's tie repeatedly, and it dawned on me that he was emulating me by wearing one.

"Juan, do you feel called to the ministry?" I asked him after service.

"Yes, I think God wants me to preach," Juan confessed, hoping that I would support him. "How did you know that, Pastor?"

"I just had a feeling," I said, eyeing his tie again. "But I think that's a good thing."

"You do?"

"Yes, I do," I said. "We need to prepare a sermon so that if an opportunity to preach arises, you'll be ready."

"That is good news, Pastor," he said grinning from ear to ear. "Will you help me prepare it?"

"Of course I will."

Days later I began teaching Juan how to prepare a sermon. He listened intently, took copious notes and asked lots of questions.

"Your testimony will be one of your strongest sermons," I told Juan. "Talk about how God changed your life. Tell people about the redemption you've experienced. Your story of faith in God and your salvation experience are the most powerful stories many people will ever hear."

Juan nodded enthusiastically.

A few weeks after our first meeting I informed Juan he would be preaching the following Sunday.

"Should I be at the church early?" he asked.

"No, Juan, that won't be necessary," I said. "You aren't going to preach at the church, you're going to preach in a market just south of Cuenca."

"In a market?"

"Yep, but that's an excellent place."

"Why's that, Pastor?"

"Because you'll be preaching to people who have never heard the gospel."

evangelism

After a Sunday service in Cuenca, Juan and I loaded a pickup truck with two boxes of New Testaments and headed for the market in Cumbe. When we arrived at the market we backed the truck up among the other vendors as if we planned on selling produce.

As I climbed out of the truck I noticed that on one side of us was a medicine man selling ointments, roots, juices and snakeskin. On the other side was a butcher midway through gutting a large pig.

"Juan, it looks like we're in good company," I said with a wink. Juan smiled nervously as the prospect of preaching in the market sank in.

We probably looked like any other vendors in the market, with the only difference being me. At 5 feet 10 inches, with blue eyes and an American heritage, I was certainly an anomaly. I was easily head and shoulders above almost everyone in the market. Being tall for once in my life felt good.

We pushed the boxes of Bibles, which Light for the Lost provided, to the tailgate and I used them for a platform. Juan's eyes followed me. Every move I made he seemed to be recording, analyzing and processing.

"I have a message for you that will change your life," I shouted to the surprise of those within earshot. Suddenly, people turned from their chores and glared at me. "It's the kind of message that'll make you a new person; it'll take away your pain and give you a new life!"

I realized I was beginning to sound like a carnival barker so I cut short my pitch and moved to my introduction of Juan.

"This young man standing next to me is Juan," I boomed. "He'll tell you the rest of the message."

As Juan stepped up onto the boxes people began to gather around the truck. I steadied Juan. He looked nervous, and I wondered if he would be able to preach.

"You'll do fine," I whispered before climbing off the truck. "Just do your best."

Juan gulped involuntarily then nodded as if he wished he had preached in a market full of nonbelievers a thousand times.

After joining the throng gathering around the truck, I noticed that Juan's legs were shaking violently. Images of him and the boxes crashing to the ground sped through my mind. But as he spoke, his voice became clear and loud. His legs stopped shaking, and his story kept drawing people to the truck.

As Juan concluded his message, I took my place at our temporary pulpit and made the altar call. It was a little bit like the altar call I heard the first time I was ever in an evangelistic church service, minus talk of the Rapture.

"If you would like a new life in Christ and to find forgiveness of your sins and the assurance of eternal life, please just slip up your hand and allow me to pray with you," I said in my best Spanish.

To be honest, I did not know exactly how well our efforts would be received. But to my surprise, every hand of those 100 or so people gathered around that truck was extended heavenward. That day we saw 100 people commit their lives to Christ. When the service was over we passed out all the Bibles we had.

The three hours we were in the market were a blur. Before we knew it, we were driving up the Pan American Highway back to Cuenca. As we did, we basked in the presence of the Lord that seemed to follow us from our evangelistic perch.

"Pastor Bill, can we come again next Sunday?" Juan asked excitedly. "It feels so good to preach, I want to do it again."

"I'd love to."

We went back to the market the following week, and the week after that, and the week after that.

Within a month we rented a house near the market and started showing the *Jesus* film. Each week the house was filled to capacity as people clambered in to hear the good news of Jesus. I realized we had enough people for an upstart church.

Today, just past the market where Juan preached for the first time, there is a thriving evangelical church. The growth of the church and all it has done since we planted it has shown me that big risks have big rewards.

And sometimes when we embrace change and take big risks for God it appears that we are dancing on the thin line that separates stupidity and blind faith.

At Unsión
we believe we have a moral duty
to influence the culture

In the world of film and television, too many Christians equate the church's lackluster attempts of the past with an unchangeable status quo. This is not the case. We can discover our role within the broadcast world and shape that role into the most powerful means of life-transformation ever seen.

If we fail to accept our responsibility in this arena, we will fulfill the dictum of English political writer Edmund Burke: All that is necessary for evil to triumph is for good men to do nothing.

My friend Craig Walters, a producer/director, puts it this way: "Christian television largely follows the philosophy that believers are only interested in spiritual programming. By ignoring the realities and interests of the outside world, great opportunities are missed. Christians have as diverse interests as those without faith. They watch sports, news, travel and entertainment, as well as spiritual and uplifting programs."

Walters has worked closely with us and has this to say about where God has taken Unsión so far:

"By mixing quality family-values programming with Bible-based teaching and ministry, Unsión is meeting their needs as well as bridging the gap to those who would never watch traditional Christian television. With nearly 25 years' background in ministry television production — including Christian networks, the Billy Graham Evangelistic Association, and other major denominations and organizations — I have been unexpectedly impressed with the excitement, energy and commitment witnessed at Unsión Television.

"I believe that if Christians are to have a continued impact in today's media," he continues. "There must be more emphasis on meeting the daily needs and interests of people as they live. Unsión Television not only meets these needs, it is a shining example of relevant Christianity today."

Is there a cost to be paid in this mission? Are there risks? Of course. But nothing worth accomplishing comes free and without risk. I love what one member of my staff recently told me: "I have no fear of dying in the Promised Land with my sword in my hand. I fear dying with my sword in my hand looking over into the Promised Land."

The very tools that have allowed a message of self-indulgence and immorality to pervade our society can be transformed into tools of soul-shaping truth. Just as Gutenberg applied the premier communications medium of his day, the printing press, to mass-produce copies of the Bible, followers of Christ can connect an audience of millions — even billions — with scriptural truth using today's media.

And scriptural truth can come in an almost infinite array of expressions once believers give full rein to the creative gifts God has given them. I look for the day when some of the most widely acknowledged film directors, producers, scriptwriters, actors, novelists, children's authors, television and radio personalities, journalists and columnists are men and women of faith who through obedience have allowed God to propel them to center stage under the media spotlights.

Their products may not — I even hope they will not — look anything like the tamed and beaten-down themes too often foisted on the public in a well-meaning but misguided attempt to share scriptural truth. No, this new generation of creative Christians will produce themes of drama, action, suspense, romance, fantasy and sci-fi that will call an audience away from the mundane and inject truth into their minds and hearts with a shock to the soul.

If they do not?

I cannot even imagine what will become of the Church.

William Fink McDonald,
(Bill's grandfather)

Richard Givan,
(Connie's dad
World War II)

Bill Sr. and Mary
McDonald (1950)

Bill Sr. and Mary McDonald

Bill

Connie

Connie (right)
and sister Lynn

Bill and Connie,
high school sweethearts

Connie and Bill

Katie

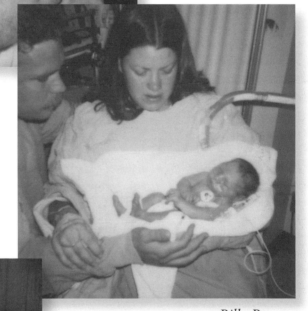
Billy Boy

Bill's Cousin, J.C., in prison

*First building rented for Christian Center on
Pan American Highway in Cuenca, Ecuador*

*First Anniversary of
Christian Center in Cuenca*

*First Baptism in
Ecuador (Maria Jose)*

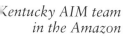
Kentucky AIM team in the Amazon

Seth and Grandfather, Dick Givan

Seth, Bill, Connie and Leah McDonald (1996 Prayer Card)

95

Bill at a church in Cañar

*Seth and Bill on
Morona River
(Amazon, Ecuador)*

*Construction of Christian
Center in Cuenca*

Baptism of a former Shuar witch doctor

Leah was home coming queen in high school

First dance at Leah and Joil's wedding

97

*Richard and
Lee Givan at their
50th Anniversary*

*Connie speaking
in Quito*

Bill and Connie (2006)

*Bill and Pastor
Jimmy Cornejo*

*Un Buen Consejo
Counseling Center*

Satellite uplink

Unsión set before the fire

*Unsión fire in Cuenca
(March 27, 2006)*

*Unsión studios
after the fire*

*Mark Lehman,
Eduardo Gonzales, and
Bill McDonald
at new Unsión
office and studios*

*Master control at
Unsión studios*

Installation of
satellite dishes.

Unsión staff

Juan Castro,
Bill McDonald and
Jimmy Cornejo

Connie and Bill at the
equator in Quito, Ecuador

Bill, Connie and Seth (2008)

Joil, Will, Drew, Leah and Emelia (2008)

Unsión antenna in Cuenca

103

ONFIDENT

One of the most challenging aspects of building a church is, well, building it. But before we could even begin to tackle that challenge we needed to find a place to build a church.

As every good Realtor will tell you, location is everything. So we looked for a prime spot. Connie and I spent many days scouting lots we could build on.

Our goal was simple: We wanted to establish a strong and influential church in the area that would attract as many people as possible. To do that, we needed to be located in a place that was visible and accessible. But we were quickly learning that such locations are hard to come by and very expensive.

Costs were prohibitive. We were in our first term as missionaries and only had funds enough to live on. In other words, we did not have much of anything to invest in a building campaign. But we did not let that fact stop us from seeking a drastic change for our church that we were sure would take it to another level.

provision

After much searching we found a wonderful piece of property — a 20,000-square-foot lot — along the Pan-American Highway. The highway is the principal road leading to and from Cuenca, so we knew we would be visible. Because the Pan-American Highway is the main artery to and from the city it also had the access we were looking for.

With confidence that I was doing God's will, I went boldly to the owner of the land and proposed a deal I thought he could not refuse.

"I want to buy this property," I said to him.

"The price is $15 a square foot."

"You want $30,000?" I asked, doing some quick math in my head.

He nodded. I sensed he was eager to sell, and knowing I did not have $30,000 in hand I determined to broker a deal that would benefit both of us.

"I don't want to release all of my money at once," I began. "So, I'd like to make payments."

The owner looked a little perplexed, but I kept talking.

"Would you take six post-dated checks for $5,000 each?" I did not wait for him to respond. "It will be like cash each month for you for six months."

The owner contemplated my offer. I am sure he did not know that the only cash I had at the time to spend on property was the $100 in my wallet. He did not need to know. I was confident, though admittedly not positive, I could raise the $5,000 each month to make good on my promise.

Some people have a problem doing business as I did that day. I realize that what I did was risky. But there is a fine line between stupidity and faith. Sometimes you have to do something that does not make sense on paper. The reason? Because you know beyond a shadow of doubt that God is in it. The purchase of the land, in my mind, was a God thing.

Don't get me wrong. I am not advocating that anyone throw his family or church into financial peril because he has an inclination to do something crazy. My motivation in writing six post-dated checks to buy a piece of land for an upstart church had more to do with remaining faithful to a call than with making a risky business decision.

faithful

When Peter stepped out of a fishing boat and walked on water, from a human point of view he did a crazy thing. Some people would even say it was a stupid thing he did. After all, he could have drowned in the stormy waters. But Peter demonstrates that there is a fine line between stupidity and faith. That fine line is whether or not God is truly calling for you to act in that manner. Peter stepped out of that boat in obedience to Jesus' command.

I believe the difference between stupidity and faith can be colossal. Stupidity requires little preparation and no prayer. Doing something on faith requires much prayer, belief that you are doing what God intended for you to do, and acting without any selfish ambition.

Buying the property the way I did, I believe, was acting in faith. Here's why. We had prayed fervently that God would lead us to the right property, I believed that purchasing the land was God's will for our church and I had heard from God so I moved upon what I had heard.

Don't get me wrong. I have crossed the stupidity line several times during the course of my life. Sometimes my ego and pride have deceived me and drawn me to places I was never called to go.

A number of years ago I read *The Man Who Could Do No Wrong*, by Charles Blair. The premise of the book is that there are many needs that must be answered, and a person can spend his entire life answering every need he comes across. However, says Blair, God did not design us to answer needs first, He designed us to answer His call on our lives first.

In my view, by purchasing the land I was actively taking part in answering God's call on my life and that of the church. And the only way I knew to buy the land was to take a giant step of faith and pray that God would provide the finances.

"Here are six checks for $5,000 each," I said as I handed the owner the checks. "At the end of each month cash each check. The funds will be there."

The owner agreed to the terms, we shook hands and I rushed home to tell Connie the good news. It's no lie that in the last weeks of every month, for the following six months after I gave the owner the checks, I had to put all my trust in God to help me raise the $5,000 to make good on my promise.

There is something exhilarating about being called to a faith decision that will bring positive change. When Peter stepped out of the boat he had no one to turn to but Jesus. I felt a similar compulsion at the end of every month. Like Peter, there were times when I began to sink.

Knowing myself as I do, if I were Peter, I would have turned and started swimming back to the boat or for the shore. But what is so intriguing about the story is that Peter's faith won't allow him to do so. Instead, he reaches out to the One who called him. He reaches out to Christ!

I like to think that Peter probably said something like, "I'm here because You called me to exercise my faith, and if You don't save me, I'm dead."

That's exactly where I found myself many times during those six months. Knowing I had willingly stepped out of the boat in faith, I knew there was no swimming back to the safety of the boat or trying to make it to shore. The only person who could really save me was Jesus.

As each deadline neared, I prayed, "I'm here because I feel You've called me. If You don't save me, I'm dead!"

I'm not proposing that taking such a risk — even if you feel it's God's will — is a good example of how to live. Surely, we can trust God for the finances we need before we sign a contract, write six post-dated checks and believe for the best.

I'm not proud that I was in such a position, and I certainly would not recommend that anyone take my experience as the standard for answering God's call on their lives or ministry. But I also believe that sometimes taking a big step for God requires us to take tremendous steps of faith, sacrifice and risk.

Within six months of turning over my post-dated checks to the owner we had paid for the land. Indeed, it was a financial miracle.

As soon as the land was paid off, we celebrated and relished God's faithfulness and goodness. But within weeks we learned another interesting lesson about God.

Sometimes He calls us to step out of the boat repeatedly — no matter how insane it may seem.

At Unsión
we believe in embracing culture

An old farmer went to market with an overloaded wagon of corn pulled by his faithful but tired mule. There, he set his corn out in neat rows on several tables he reserved. Within minutes he had propped up his hand-painted sign advertising: "Sweet Corn, By the Ear, By the Bushel."

All around the farmer were other farmers. The first thing he noticed was they were not just selling corn. He was flanked by every variety of garden vegetable and orchard fruit he ever imagined. His corn was not as special as he thought. In fact, it was just part of the mix.

What do you think would happen if that farmer decided he did not want his corn in such a pluralistic environment? What if that farmer decided selling corn within sight of piles of potatoes and carrots and apples just would not do? What if he insisted on a corn-only arena for his sales?

He would soon be looking for other employment.

But that is how a lot of Christians view the evangelistic use of television or other media. They insist on niche programming, on an uninterrupted schedule of preaching and gospel singing and Christian talk shows featuring Christian hosts and Christian guests discussing Christian topics in fluent Christianese.

I am convinced you cannot truly impact a lost world through niche television programming. At Unsión we aim to go into the marketplace. We offer programming that injects Christian values even when theology is not the subject. Our example is no less than Jesus himself.

The Lord did not cloister himself in synagogues. He went to the masses. He was on warm personal terms with people from all walks of life. That is how He communicated the Kingdom. Jesus nurtured His disciples through everyday interaction. Through the intimacy of meals and sailing together on the Sea of Galilee and coming as a guest to their homes, Jesus used life to make theology come alive.

Perhaps His most effective teaching tool within those everyday encounters was His parables. Jesus told stories that created bridges between people's concrete life experiences and the seeming intangibles of heaven. At Unsión we strive to produce programming that will be popular, yet carry spiritual truth. We call it "popular parable programming."

Most educators agree moral standards are established through storytelling. Go back 2,400 years to one of history's premier teachers, Plato, and you will find him calling for stories, music and art that influence children to fall in love with virtue and hate vice.

Why stories? Why not simply explain the difference between right and wrong to your children? Why not supply them with a list of dos and don'ts? Because people remember stories better than they remember rules and regulations.

Think of that word, imagination. It comes from "image," a mental picture. When a moral principle has the power to move us into action, it is often because it is backed up by a picture or image.

I believe much of today's storytelling has moved from the printed page. Our culture is being shaped by story, yes. The masses are determining whether they will pursue vice or virtue. But the messengers influencing those decisions are more often coming into the home through the airwaves.

Don't kid yourself. Today's media moguls, producers and writers have a major overriding goal — influencing culture.

"Those who have the mass media in their hands ... bear responsibility for the world and for the future of humanity," said former Czech Republic President Vaclav Havel in 1995 during a commencement address at Harvard University. "Just as the splitting of the atom can immensely enrich humanity in a thousand and one ways and, at the same time, can also threaten it with destruction, so television can have both good and evil consequences. Quickly, suggestively, and to an unprecedented degree, it can disseminate the spirit of understanding, humanity, human solidarity and spirituality, or it can stupefy whole nations and continents. And just as our use of atomic energy depends solely on our sense of responsibility, so the proper use of television depends on our sense of responsibility as well."

Most people in the Western world prior to 9/11 would have been unfamiliar with the Arab media conglomerate Al Jazeerah. But as our awareness of the Muslim world dramatically increased with the tragic events of 2001, Western media sources took note of these communicators who seemed to have direct access to Osama Bin Laden's periodic messages.

Al Jazeerah is now producing an English news channel. They have one goal — to shape your worldview! Their plan is to change the way your children think, live and believe. They envision a day when your grandchildren will worship Allah, and they plan to bring about that day through mass media.

Al Jazeerah is entering into an incredible battle for viewers. They are competing against major networks that tower over their strength, abilities and reach. Yet, they see that battle as their mandate, their reason for being.

Some battles are fought not because they can be won, but because they are perceived to be just. There are countless organizations with their own agendas and philosophies they are willing to uphold at all cost. Al Jazeerah is only one example.

And in this mix, Christian broadcasters can continue to circle the wagons and preach to the choir, or they can become communications innovators who impact their culture.

It is up to us.

POSSIBILITIES

Church was over, and we lingered in the sanctuary chatting with congregants as we usually did. In Ecuador there usually isn't a mass exodus the moment a service ends because Ecuadorians see church and all things related to it as experiences to be savored. Time, it seems, does not matter.

But as the last of the congregation flittered out of the sanctuary, I grabbed my Bible and headed for the car. Before I could step out the door one of the women in the church who was a longtime worshipper with us stopped me.

"Pastor, I hesitate to tell you this, but I must," she said. "Last night I was praying for you and your family and God gave me a vision."

I politely listened not exactly sure what to expect.

"God showed me a vision of you holding a baby boy," she continued. "He was a happy baby who had blonde hair and blue eyes."

As soon the words left the woman's mouth, I was stunned. What no one but our closest confidants knew was that Connie was contemplating tubal ligation reversal because she too felt that God had given her a vision.

"God is going to bless us with a blonde-haired, blue-eyed boy," Connie had told me weeks earlier.

"Honey, where are we going to adopt such a baby in Ecuador?" I asked, trying to be as sensitive to her feelings and needs as possible, but still wanting to stay grounded in the reality of our situation.

"We aren't going to adopt," Connie said. "We're going to get pregnant."

I did not want to lose any more babies, and the thought of Connie's life at risk absolutely terrified me.

Shortly after Katie died we decided to have no more children. Doing so was another heartbreak for both of us. Ever since I had known Connie she had said her only dream in life was to be a wife and mother. Though she ached to have more children, she had her tubes tied and for several years we toyed with the idea of adopting a baby.

With Connie telling me she wanted to get pregnant, I could not help but think of the sorrow we went through after Billy and Katie died. I vividly remember after Katie died when Connie told me she had very little to live for. There was no way I wanted to go through those dark times again.

"Connie, you had the surgery. That can't be reversed," I said. "Plus, the doctors said if you ever became pregnant you have less than a 20 percent chance of having a healthy baby."

"But God showed me in a dream that we're going to have a blonde-haired, blue-eyed baby," she said. "And, yes, the tubal ligation can be reversed. I have been researching it and found a doctor here in Quito who was trained in the States to do that."

For several weeks we went back and forth discussing whether or not she should get the reversal. I had many concerns. The first being that the doctor Connie had found had never actually performed a tubal ligation reversal in Ecuador. The second being that if the surgery was a success, what would happen if Connie became pregnant?

believe

I sought the counsel of trusted friends. Elmer Bueno, a fellow missionary and mentor, told me if Connie felt sincerely that she had heard from the Lord and wanted to move forward with the surgery I should not stand in the way. I considered his words and the advice of other friends. With much prayer I came to the conclusion that I had to trust God and Connie.

Weeks later Connie underwent the reversal. About three months later she was pregnant. When she told me the news I felt as if I could float. Neither of us was afraid. We had complete peace and absolutely believed that God was walking with us.

Three months into the pregnancy Connie began to show signs of an impending miscarriage. I rushed her to the doctor. After his exam he spoke with me privately and informed me that he wanted to abort the baby.

"If we don't abort the baby, your wife could die," he said. "Her blood pressure is off the charts."

I knew Connie would not believe she was going to die. I also knew that if I told her what she was facing it would only make the situation worse. After prayer and counsel with a couple of our dearest friends I decided not to tell Connie that the doctor wanted to abort the baby.

That may sound terrible, but I was positive Connie would not consider an abortion, and telling her would only exacerbate the situation. For the next six months the doctors and I monitored every move Connie made.

As the pregnancy reached its ninth month, I grew somewhat concerned that the baby might be microcephalic, but trusted God he would not be.

On June 30, 1992, Seth Xavier McDonald was born. As Connie had seen in her vision, he was healthy and had blonde hair and blue eyes.

In a very good way our lives would never be the same.

At Unsión
we believe in being fearless

What is holding us back? That is a question I constantly ask myself.

Are we afraid of powerful cultural forces that intimidate us? Are we scared of failure? Could we simply fear being exposed for who we are?

Like the doubting spies who journeyed into Canaan and reported back to Moses, many times followers of Christ get sidetracked by focusing on the giants life throws at us when we should be readying ourselves to defeat the forces of evil. The spies looked at their own strength and could only forecast failure and defeat, while God was waiting — or at least wanting — to bring the victory. I do not want to be like the spies. God wants to join our fights, and I am going to let Him.

There is no greater saga of giant-slaying than that of David and Goliath. But read that narrative in 1 Samuel 17 and you will find the real action follows a long waiting period in which not much happened. Israel and the Philistines had taken their battle positions. For 40 days the army of Israel lived in fear of Goliath — the Philistines' champion. On all fronts it was a gut-wrenching stalemate with no victory in sight.

Sometimes we live with giants God did not create us to live with. Television wants to dictate what we say, do, buy and believe. Major religions want to influence your children through every available media outlet. Because of it, Christ's followers must be vigilant.

We don't fight battles because we can win them; we fight them because they have to be fought. Why does a father take on an armed intruder? He does not calculate the fight or count the costs; he simply says he will not let his family be violated. But the wonderful reality for the Christ follower is we don't rely on ourselves to achieve victory.

We have the responsibility to get into the fight for our future, our culture, our worldview, our faith and the faith of our children and grandchildren. It looks to be a fight that is impossible. Too many are tempted to fall back and passively allow the power brokers and culture changers to take the reins of our faith. But God is waiting to step into the fray with those communicators who will trust Him and proclaim a Kingdom message.

Israel came up against a giant, and sadly they had begun to live with a giant. The Scriptures say they had taken their stand on the battlefield for 40 days. When David saw the situation, he could not live with the giant's threat. It was a battle every soldier in Israel's army was convinced he could not win. What hope was there for a teen-age shepherd?

But David refused to look at Goliath through the lens of his own ability. He put that giant next to God and discovered an infinite size difference.

Goliath had put his finger in Israel's faces. He threatened them, accused them, and promised to take their lives. It is an Old Testament saga with plenty of parallels for a New Testament church.

Like Israel, we take our stand, we call out our message, but we are living with things that want to destroy us. Satan, like Goliath, has plenty of his messengers with their fingers wagging in the faces of Christ's followers. "I want your life, I want your testimony, and I want your peace! I want your family, I want your children, and I want your home!"

God did not create us to live with giants; God created us to slay giants. David came on the scene incredulous at the lack of faith he saw among his brethren.

"What is this all about?" he demands. "Why are you doing this? You are living with the giant! You are living with a thing that is threatening you, that's robbing from you! You are living with something that's going to destroy you."

Everyone's giant is different. Maybe your giant is a sin that wants to rob you of your testimony, a habit that wants to rob you of your integrity, an attitude that wants to rob you of your peace, an appetite that wants to rob you of your spirituality, a fear that wants to rob you of your future, or a confusion that wants to rob you of your vision.

David says, "I'm not going to live with this. I'll take on that giant. I'm not going to stay behind the line. I'm not going to be content to shout empty insults at the enemy. I'm going to kill myself a giant!"

David undertook his mission in the midst of the doubt around him. When he approached King Saul with the offer to do battle with the enemy, he was met with incredulity.

"But you're just a boy!" the fearful king insisted.

I love that part of the story. Isn't that the way it is when we step out in faith? When we want to take on something bigger than ourselves, there is always someone — and sometimes it is the best of people — who says, "You really can't do that. We've never been able to do that! You don't have the education for it, you don't have the money for it, you don't have the fortitude for it, and you don't have the support for it. We've never been able to lick that giant. You can't beat that giant."

We cannot forget that in one respect Saul was absolutely right. David could not defeat that giant. It was impossible to beat that giant unless God showed up.

Nothing has changed. God is looking for men and women and young people to take on battles they cannot win without God.

When we were first married, Connie and I had a crazy miniature dachshund. Anyone with a miniature dachshund understands the adjective "crazy." We were at the park one day and encountered a Chow Chow that looked like a lion or bear roaming suburbia. Inexplicably, my little wiener dog decided to attack the Chow Chow.

My wife and I looked at each other in amazement as that wiener dog flew into the face of the Chow Chow. You would have thought our dog owned the park. The Chow Chow grabbed my miniature dachshund and began to treat it like a dishrag, chomping her by the neck and slamming her around, her 2-inch legs flailing! But whenever our dachshund broke loose, vroom, she was flying back toward the much bigger dog. Then the Chow Chow nabbed my dog mid-air and went for the kill. My dog had taken on a fight she could not win.

I stepped in and put a death grip on the Chow Chow. I pulled its mouth open and shook my little dog out. That was one fight I would never have involved myself in if it had not been for my wiener dog. Why did I get in that fight? Because my dog took on a fight she could not win.

God is waiting for some of us to be like that wiener dog. He wants us to take on some fights we cannot win on our own. And when we catch that whiff of spiritual adrenaline and obediently place ourselves in the path of satanic attack and apparent destruction, He will show up! God did not create us to live with giants; He created us to slay them.

At our studios we slay giants every day. Recently, as I walked through the studio I saw some of our hosts doing a craft show. In the control room I saw workers giving cameramen direction and editing programs that will be saved to a hard drive then placed on a server for distribution. I am amazed that all of this happens for just $100 an hour — peanuts in mass communications terms. For only $73,000 a month we are putting together another installment of our popular parable programming. In the television business money is always an issue. Currently, Unsión lives hand to mouth depending greatly on advertisers, but especially donors.

Some months I feel like David at the beginning of his battle with Goliath. Each and every hour of the day we are taking on giants such as Univision. Such networks want our viewers. Every day we encounter new growing pains. But it is worth it. Every day more than 100,000 people watch our craft show. I smile when I envision 3 million people watching the network at any given moment.

We have stepped into a battle it looked like we could never win. When times get tough the only thing that gives us comfort is that we know we have the ultimate Giant Killer on our side.

FUL

With the property secured and in the name of the national church we moved ahead with plans to build the church. Once again, we did not have the finances to do so. But that did not stop me from believing God wanted us to have a church home of our own.

Figuring I had nothing to lose, I commissioned the most renowned engineer in Cuenca to draw up plans for our church. He drew a beautiful, 1,000-seat sanctuary. Though the plan was only to get the church drawn, everything changed once we had the blueprints in hand.

The possibilities of having our own place of worship played on my mind. But the fact we did not have the money to break ground kept bringing me back to the reality of our situation.

Even so, I was thrilled to have property and blueprints. But my good feelings were short lived. The engineer called and gave me some very unexpected news.

"Bill, the ground you want to build on is unstable," he said. "You're going to need to dig huge footers so that whatever you build on that property will be able to withstand the tremors and earthquakes that are common here in Cuenca."

"Are such huge footings necessary?"

"If you want a stable building, they are."

"When we break ground that'll be the first thing we'll do," I said, not sure what I was committing to. "We'll follow your lead on this."

I know just a little about construction, but even a novice like me knows that the least expensive part of the job in Ecuador was getting big holes dug to secure the foundation. And once again, I believed our congregation and my fund-raising could get the financing in place to pay for the labor to dig the holes and construct the footers.

After we had raised a few thousand dollars, crews began digging the 18 holes we needed. The engineer said the holes needed to be 6 feet by 6 feet and 6 feet deep. When the holes were dug they were filled with rocks, steel and concrete.

If you've ever built a house you know the strange mix of trepidation and excitement that accompanies going to your lot and seeing what has been completed at the end of each week. As I walked around the lot inspecting 18 patches of concrete, I could not help but feel fearful. Had I wasted the church's money and been duped by the engineer?

"After all that work, time and money, this is all we have to show for it?" I asked Connie. "We just buried $9,000 in the earth."

committed

I put the project on hold as I raised money. Unexpectedly, the funds came in faster than I could have imagined, and we began to build columns for the structure. But as soon as the first column went up, the criticism began pouring in.

"You're overbuilding this church," spat one man.

"All these safety precautions are a waste of money," said another man. "We don't build like this in Ecuador."

Some people even accused me of being duped by the engineer. The criticism that hurt the most, though, and even made me angry was when people would say I had wasted the church's funds. One member even called me a crazy gringo.

I weathered the verbal salvos and prayed the engineer's advice was accurate. Because we had limited funds, we built a third of the first floor at a time. As soon as we had a roof we moved our services into the church — despite not having any walls or plumbing.

Within months of moving under the roof, Cuenca was rattled repeatedly by a string of tremors. Throughout the city many buildings were damaged because they did not have sufficient footers. To my delight our building did not move, crack or sway. In fact, it suffered no damage. This proved my detractors wrong, and a handful of them even began referring to me as the wise gringo.

I am the first to admit I am not the wisest man when it comes to church construction. But I did and do understand that a quality foundation is one of the cornerstones to a strong building.

The ridicule I received for the construction of the footers was nothing compared to the despair and regret I would later feel when my friend Peter fell off the roof of the church and died. Peter's death was very disturbing. Wrapping my mind around the fact that such a good man had died while doing something for the church was hard to comprehend.

David Thomas, a fellow missionary and good friend of mine,

told me a story that helped me put Peter's death in perspective. Thomas told me that the great cathedrals and basilicas of Europe were not valued on the amount of money invested in them, but were valued instead on the number of deaths incurred during construction. According to Thomas, in some cases more than 1,000 workers died in the construction of such basilicas and cathedrals. His point to me was that great vision requires even greater sacrifice.

Peter paid the ultimate price while helping establish our church and other ministries. But his efforts were not in vain. Christian Center has been growing steadily for almost two decades now. Today more than 4,000 people attend the church. Adjacent to it are a Christian school and Bible college. At least 100 people per week come to Christ through the ministries of the church.

Because of it, I believe each person who comes to Christ will add a jewel into Peter's eternal crown in heaven.

"Do not store up for yourselves treasures on earth, where moth and rust destroy, and where thieves break in and steal. But store up for yourselves treasures in heaven, where moth and rust do not destroy, and where thieves do not break in and steal" *(Matthew 6:19,20).*

At Unsión
we believe the impossible is possible

More times than not, our greatest hurdles in achieving great things happen in our mind. As someone once said, the world's greatest battles were not at Gettysburg, Normandy or Waterloo; they take place every day in the space between people's ears.

I am convinced that God did not choose Connie and me to found Unsión because we are super-talented, intelligent or smooth operators. In fact, I think He chose us because we lack so many of those coveted qualities.

If I had understood the risk, sacrifice and struggle Unsión would require, I know I would have shied away from the opportunity. Most people would. When we start adding up the costs, imagining all that can go wrong, comparing ourselves to others and trying to figure out how everything is going to work out, we become our own worst enemies.

When Connie and I were pastoring our first church in Lexington, Kentucky, a strange though not unusual phenomenon occurred — instead of our congregation growing, we lost people.

After one particularly brutal board meeting, I went home absolutely convinced I needed to resign. *The church will be better off without me* ran the endless refrain through my head.

I fell onto our couch and let the despair welling inside me engulf me like a wave. Self-pity was suddenly my constant companion. I decided that I needed a "Word from the Lord," and I did something that I would not recommend any sane person to do. I decided I would allow the Bible to fall open where it may and then, with eyes closed, I would blindly point to a Scripture with my index finger to find out what God wanted to tell me.

Sure enough my finger landed squarely on something I could hang onto, "Be unmovable". It was a good word, but my despair was greater than my faith so I decided to play my game of Bible roulette again.

This time the verse was not as promising, so I laughed out loud and quickly came to my senses. I figured if God was playing my little game He must have a sense of humor too.

"I don't have the ability to pastor this church!" I said to no one in particular.

It was not long before Connie came home and asked why I was in a funk. I tried to explain to her how low I felt.

With little visible sympathy, she grabbed me by the collar and boldly said, "Billy, God is not looking for a man with ability; He is looking for a man with availability!"

Her words banished my ill feelings immediately. When I told her how I felt, I really wanted her to agree with me that I was probably the worst leader she had ever known. Instead, she was telling me to pull myself up by the bootstraps, do my best and let God deal with the rest.

Connie's words came to me as prophetic and have guided my life and ministry ever since. The encounter also taught me that self-pity is not only egotistical; it also can kill our availability.

So, why did God choose me to found Unsión? Simple! Because I was available. To do great things for God we have to start with being available. When we have conquered that giant, there are others that will require God's coming to our defense. When He does, we can overcome any obstacles — even those that seem insurmountable.

EVOLVING

As Christian Center continued to grow and nationals were trained for leadership, I sensed God was prompting me to transition to another ministry. The problem was, I was not sure what ministry He was leading me to. But when I stumbled on an opportunity of a lifetime, the course of my ministry and life changed.

In 2002 a friend offered to sell me a television frequency, saying it could be used as a ministry tool. I was skeptical at first. Plus, I had never produced television programs, let alone run a network. In truth, founding a television network was the farthest thing from my mind.

But as I prayed about it and discussed it with my ministry team, I came to the conclusion God wanted us to buy the rights to the frequency, but only if we could raise the necessary $50,000 by the deadline we had been given.

To my surprise, the money poured in. Before I knew it, we owned a television frequency. What I did not know at the time is that we would eventually have to raise and invest more than $1 million to build the station and complete the infrastructure.

One of our goals in getting into television was to provide an alternative to the often violent and sexually explicit programming on other channels in Cuenca. But we also wanted to use our time on the air to minister to people.

"Even the tiniest shacks have an antenna sticking out of the roof," I told a reporter from the United States when word got out that we were getting into the television business. "With this station we can go into homes where we otherwise wouldn't be invited through the front door."

From Unsión's earliest days we have used the station to broadcast a variety of teaching, musical and dramatic programs. During commercials we run advertisements packed with Christian values and ethics.

We also offer programs such as *Touched by an Angel* and *7th Heaven*, nature and geographic documentaries, and a magazine show that highlights local people and events.

In addition to the family-friendly programming, we include 30-minute segments from Christian Center, which Connie and I eventually turned over to national pastors Jimmy and Aida Cornejo.

Out of that lineup, some of the most effective evangelism tools we broadcast are those 30-second commercial-like spots on such themes as hope, unity, forgiveness and the power of prayer. During these commercials we include a number on the screen directing viewers to call our counseling center, Un Buen Consejo (Good Advice), to talk with counselors and receive prayer.

In Unsión's early years we only had 10 employees, a handful of volunteers and some excellent donations from faithful supporters. I was extremely impressed and grateful we could produce such a quality product with our limited funds, technology and staff.

On all fronts our staff was diligent and faithful with the little things God had given us. Because of it, I believe, God decided to take us to another level where we would have the opportunity to share the gospel with hundreds of millions of people.

And it would all start one day with a stranger at my door.

miraculous

When I answered the door, a well-dressed man extended his hand toward me and told me his name was Byron Pachecho. He was cordial and intelligent. I had little to fear and was glad to make a new friend.

"Good to meet you, Mr. Pachecho, how can I help you?" I said, still a little taken aback by his unannounced visit.

"I need your help," he said after we spent several minutes chit-chatting. "Someone told me you pray for sick people."

Pachecho then informed me his sister was in the hospital with cancer. The family was at a loss as to what to do, as the doctors had given a grim prognosis.

"I can't heal your sister," I said. "But I know who can."

Soon after my meeting with Pachecho I sent Eduardo Gonzales, executive president of the network, to the hospital to pray with Pachecho's sister. A few weeks later, there was another knock at our apartment door. When I answered it, Pachecho was beaming.

"My sister has been miraculously healed with no medical intervention," he said. "And because of this miracle our family has been restored."

As we talked, Pachecho told me he was the president of the Ecuadorian Cable Association. I thought that was a happy coincidence, but what he said next almost floored me.

"I would like to put Unsión Television on every cable system in Ecuador," he said.

"That sounds great," I heard myself say, though I had no idea what that would eventually mean to me. "What will that entail?"

"You'll need to purchase a satellite signal."

I met with our board and informed them of Pachecho's offer. We agreed to investigate the offer. The first thing we learned was that buying a satellite signal was pricey. The second thing we learned was that a satellite signal gave us the ability to reach 500 million Spanish-speakers throughout the world. That fact sold us on the deal immediately.

God was with us as word spread that we were contemplating acquiring a satellite signal, Speed the Light, a ministry that buys vehicles and equipment for missionaries, offered to buy all the necessary equipment.

After brief negotiations, a satellite company agreed to handle our signal. Within a few short months we were on 50 cable systems across Ecuador. But that was just the beginning.

By moving from a local channel to satellite, we were thrust into a cutthroat market where rival networks want nothing more than for their competition to fail. But it is also a market where marketers are willing to pay top dollar to reach viewers. We also discovered that through Unsión we could become an influence on the culture with the programming we provided.

I regularly tell people that each faith-based commercial we produce is seen millions of times. The cost to us to produce and broadcast one of our homespun, but high-quality, commercials is a paltry $1,000. That means it costs just pennies to put the gospel message in front of our viewers multiple times.

In doing so, we believe, there have been eternal dividends. Since Unsión has been on the air, more than 45,000 individuals have made contact with our counseling center and professed a decision for Christ.

That is exactly why we exist — to see people come to an understanding of Jesus Christ so that they will embrace Him as their Savior.

At Unsión
we believe in miracles

A few years ago my friend Marty Hensley came to Unsión for a visit. As we visited the sets and pre- and post-production facilities he blurted, "This is a miracle!"

I smiled at the thought. Though I had seen God open many doors and work through Unsión on many occasions, I had never thought of the network as being a miracle. Honestly, I usually thought of it as being a lot of hard work that — in spite of me — reaped huge eternal dividends.

"I guess it does look like a miracle," I said, but I was really thinking: *If this is a miracle, how come it's so stinkin' hard?*

The answer I eventually arrived at was reinforced by a couple of Bible stories I have read countless times. The first was that of the Virgin Birth.

An innocent Jewish girl finds herself talking to angels and then becoming pregnant. Then she has to explain to her family that she is pregnant even though she is still a virgin. I can only guess that Mary said at some point, "If this is a miracle, how come it's so stinkin' hard?"

Then I was reminded of the story of the Exodus in the Old Testament. Israel is finally set free from 400 years of bondage in Egypt. But as they make their way towards the Promised Land the trip is less than easy. They are in the desert, at first trailed by the Egyptian army and then living on manna they have to believe will reappear each day. Their miracle of deliverance is so hard that some of them even grumbled that they would just as soon live as slaves than to live through the divine liberation.

I am sure some of them said, "If this is a miracle, how come it's so stinkin' hard?"

Many of the miracles and great events recorded in the Bible were preceded by tragic and trying times. Christ's resurrection is a great example. Leading up to the Resurrection there is a trail of doubt, betrayal, fear, confusion, bloodshed and even the Lord's death.

At one point Christ says, *"My Father, if it is possible, may this cup be taken from me. Yet not as I will, but as you will"* (Matthew 26:39).

Walking through the process of building a television network, I have learned something about miracles. The main lesson about miracles I have learned is that they do not come easily. In fact, some of them require sacrifice, trials, hurt and pain. But they also require faith, patience, unyielding trust and a desire to follow God's will no matter what the odds. Obviously it takes faith to see the hand of God move on our behalf.

"And without faith it is impossible to please God, because anyone who comes to him must believe that he exists and that he rewards those who earnestly seek him" (Hebrews 11:6).

Tenacity is an important ingredient in any faith endeavor. We hear from God; we respond by taking steps of faith to fulfill His will. During the entire journey we should expect to be challenged by failure, doubt and even persecution.

Over the years, many people have asked me what the keys to successful ministry are. I tell each person the same thing, "Hang in there, respond to what you have heard and keep responding."

It is really that simple; it is really that hard.

One evening I came home from a national church leaders meeting, and I felt I had not been treated fairly. For the first time in my life I felt I was a victim of prejudice. I was so hurt and disappointed I told Connie, "I quit; we're moving back to the States!"

Connie looked at me sideways and said, "Billy, don't talk to me about going anywhere until God has talked to you about going somewhere!" Again, in an instant, Connie's words came to me as prophetic. Many such conversations with Connie stand as guideposts to my life and ministry.

Most of us make greater mistakes for leaving too soon than for staying too long. If we hear from God, then circumstances and feelings should not dissuade us from the direction God has given us.

I will keep moving in the direction I feel God has called me to go until I am called in a new direction. Faith, tenacity, steadfastness, bullheadedness, resolve, resolution, persistence and determination are sometimes the only things that will keep us on the course God has given us.

142

SUPERNATURAL

Eduardo Gonzalez, our station manager, came into a staff meeting one day and wanted to share a story in the middle of a very intense planning session.

I thought to myself, *Well this is no time to be telling stories.*

Eduardo was undeterred and went on to say that just the day before he was in the morning service at our home church in Cuenca, and during the altar call he went forward to pray with a gentleman about his same age who had made his way to the altar for salvation.

Eduardo introduced himself to the man to make him feel at home and to encourage him in his newfound faith.

"What is your name?" Eduardo asked.

"Miguel."

Then Eduardo inquired as to how he happened to come to our church in Cuenca that morning.

Miguel replied, "The craziest thing happened last night. I could not sleep, so I turned on the TV, and during the middle of an interesting program I saw a commercial. It was an advertisement encouraging me to call a local number to talk about some issues that I was struggling with. So I called, and the person prayed with me and invited me to church."

Eduardo explained to Miguel that he worked for Unsión and that our network existed to bring Christian-values programming as an alternative to the often violent and sexually explicit fare on the other channels in Cuenca.

"That is a good thing," Miguel said. "I needed to see what I saw last night."

"I am the station manager at Unsión, and I am so pleased that we were able to help you," Eduardo said. "Whom did you speak with at our counseling center?"

Miguel responded, "I spoke with someone by the name of Jeff."

"Jeff? We don't have anyone on our staff named Jeff. What time did you call our center?"

"About 2:30 a.m."

"I am sorry, but you must be mistaken for we have no one on our staff by the name of Jeff, and our last counselor goes home at midnight," Eduardo said.

Miguel insisted he had the name and time right. "If I did not talk to Jeff at 2:30 a.m. last night, then please tell me how I am in church this morning?"

Eduardo was at a loss for words.

We will never know whom Miguel spoke to or why he tuned in to our channel, called the counseling center and made his way to our church the next morning. All we know is that a young man was prompted to come to church and receive Christ as his Savior after tuning in to Unsión on his television.

God does work in mysterious ways.

At Unsión
we believe we can
reach millions of Hispanic viewers

As I said earlier, Unsión exists to shape culture so that we can direct Hispanic viewers to a relationship with Jesus Christ. To some — especially Hollywood-types — it may come as a surprise that there are millions of people who want quality entertainment without the sexuality, crudeness and violence. It is those people we will probably reach first, as they are seeking us as much as we are seeking them.

A prime example of this is a group of church members in Calle, Colombia, who approached their local cable company and asked if Unsión was available in the area. They were told it was not, but if they wanted it to be considered for broadcast they needed 25,000 signatures.

The small church embraced the challenge and set out to collect the signatures. Members of the congregation returned to the cable company a few months later with the required signatures. Today, 80,000 homes in Calle receive the Unsión signal.

One of the most exciting things about Unsión is its potential. There are a vast number of Ecuadorians and Spanish speakers in Europe and the United States. Because of our satellites we have the ability to reach almost all of them and tens of millions of others.

Reports indicate more than 850,000 Ecuadorians live in New York City and New Jersey. More than 400,000 of them are from the area surrounding Cuenca. When we learned that, we began broadcasting in New York on a digital station.

Already our counseling center has six locations with hundreds of trained staff members working the phones. Viewers often report how thankful they are for the family-values programming from a Christian worldview that we provide.

Yes, we believe we can reach the Spanish-speaking world — one person at a time — with wholesome entertainment and Christ's message of love and grace embedded in the programming. As a matter of fact, we feel it is our duty to do so.

After all, we have been commissioned by Christ to tell the greatest story ever told.

SIVE

Several years before I founded Unsión, a woman slid into the back row of Christian Center. She would teach me a great lesson that would give me fuel when Unsión faced seemingly insurmountable odds.

The little woman kept her head down as she waited for service to start. I had not seen her before and wondered if her timid nature was the reason why. Wanting to be sure anyone visiting our church connected with at least one person, I made my way over to her and introduced myself.

"Hi, I'm Pastor Bill," I said in Spanish, extending my hand toward her.

The woman did not look up and made no eye contact with me. As we shook hands she mumbled something, but her voice was so soft and low I did not hear what she had said.

"What's your name?" I asked.

"Betty." Her reply was almost inaudible, but I was encouraged to know that at least she spoke.

"Well, Betty, we're glad to have you in service tonight," I said. "I hope you enjoy it."

Betty nodded and kept her seat on the back row of the church. I headed for the front of the church, hoping I did not embarrass her or make her feel uncomfortable. At the close of my sermon I gave an altar call. To my surprise, Betty was the first one to the altar.

One of our ladies prayed with her. When service was dismissed, Betty stuck around and waited to talk with me. I asked her how she arrived at the church that night, and she began to tell me her story.

She said she had come to the end of life's rope and that she had decided it would be better to end her life rather than live in her present condition. In that state of mind she ran into a friend in the city who told her, "You should give that church in town a chance before doing anything drastic."

Betty said she came to our church as a last resort.

"Tonight I have found a reason to live," she told me. "Tonight I've found Christ as my Lord and Savior."

Connie and I embraced Betty. We were so pleased to celebrate her conversion. The next Sunday Betty came to church. For several weeks she rushed to the altar every time I gave an altar call for those who wanted to accept Christ as Savior.

called

One evening I knelt next to Betty just to hear what she was praying about. I was surprised to hear that she was not praying for herself and her tremendous needs. Instead, she was praying the simplest prayer: "Lord, help me win souls for You."

I was astounded. Here was a frail, timid woman who had many needs, and she was praying that God would use her to win souls for Him.

As we discipled Betty and she grew in her relationship with

the Lord, it became evident she was determined to tell others about Jesus.

"Pastor Bill, please send me to preach the gospel to the Cañaries," she said one evening.

I considered her request. The Cañaries were known as difficult people to reach with the gospel. They are an indigenous group who primarily live in the town of Cañar a couple of hours north of Cuenca. All of the attempts I knew of to evangelize them had failed.

"Betty, you're a new believer," I started. "The Cañaries are a difficult people. Seasoned ministers have failed to reach them with the gospel. I'd be more comfortable seeing you minister to people who were more open to Jesus."

Though my words were diplomatic, inside I was thinking, *Come on, Betty, you are too bashful and shy. How could you ever carry the gospel to such a hard and gospel-resistant city?*

Betty took my words in stride. But every service she raced to the altar to pray. As I prayed at the altars I could usually hear her praying, "Jesus help me win Cañaries for You."

At the close of every service she would make her way over to me and ask when I was going to send her to preach the gospel to the Cañaries.

This went on for months, and my answer did not change.

"Betty, you're just not ready."

One evening she made her way to me. I was prepared to give my pat answer, but before I could even form words she said, "I have a new question for you. If you won't send me, who will you send?"

She had my attention. She had worn me out, and I heard myself tell her that if she could find someone to go with her, she could go to the Cañaries and tell them about Jesus. The next day we bought her a bus ticket, gave her some Bibles and some tracts and sent her along with "Little Cloud" (or Nubecita in Spanish), another Christian woman in our church, for a few days to minister to the Cañaries.

The next Sunday Betty was eager to share with me the events of her trip to Cañar. She said that when they boarded the bus her friend took one seat available in the front. In the back of the bus was another seat next to a man. After an hour or so, the man left and another man took the seat beside Betty.

As she rode along, she told me, she had her Bible on her lap and she was praying the same prayer she had prayed so many times before: "Jesus, give me the souls of Cañaries."

Eventually the man seated next to her spoke up. "Excuse me," he asked, "but what is that black book in your lap?"

Betty said boldness came over her that she had never known.

"I looked him squarely in the eyes," Betty recalled. "I lifted my Bible and said, 'Sir, this is the Word of God, and in this Book you will find forgiveness of your sins and find eternal life!'"

Betty said she continued to preach, and after her short discourse the man began to cry.

"I am sorry, sir, did I offend you?" Betty asked.

"Oh, no, you did not offend me," he replied. "Last night I had a dream, and in my dream a lady came to me with a black book and she told me that the book held the secret of forgiveness of sins and eternal life." After a pause, he added, "You're the woman from my dream."

Betty then led the man in the sinner's prayer. When the bus reached Cañar, the man thanked her and said goodbye.

"Are you from this town?"

"Of course I am," the man replied. "I am a Cañari."

An hour later Betty planted herself on a bench in the city's park. She placed her Bible on her lap and waited for someone to come along and take a seat next to her so she could witness. Betty made the trip a weekly occurrence.

Eventually she asked me to go with her to see her "work." The day I traveled to Cañar there were around 100 people waiting for her at the park. Since then, Betty has pioneered four churches and today leads a congregation of more than 1,000 people.

Besides persistence, I learned something else from Betty — God can use anyone to do anything as long as he or she is willing and available.

At Unsión
we believe in taking calculated risks

Few adventures come without risk. Maybe that is why we call risky expeditions adventures. The New Testament is full of people taking risks. But Peter sticks out in my mind as one of the greatest risk takers of all time. He steps out of a boat during a violent storm to be near Christ.

I can only guess, but it appears that Peter wants more, he wants an adventure, he wants to explore, and he wants to take a risk.

It is hard not to be mesmerized by the idea of people walking on water. But to stop there is to miss the point. The theme of the story is man's obedience while taking a great risk.

To be honest, there are times when complete faith can look strikingly similar to stupidity. But when God calls us to do something, it does not matter what the world thinks.

Yes, our faith may make us look stupid to people who have not experienced Jesus, but to those of us who have, we know His calls to acts of faith — even outrageous ones — are transformative and part of a bigger picture.

My call to start a television network is connected to my call to missions, which is connected to my call to ministry, which is connected to my salvation experience. What is the main thing connecting all these things together? Jesus. And He is the One who keeps calling me to take risks for Him.

As I do, He continues to prove himself faithful. My job is not to go looking for risks. Instead, it is to embrace them when God presents them.

As Peter walks across the water, he begins to sink. No surprise there; taking risks is not without danger. But when we take God-given risks, Jesus reaches down, like He did with Peter, and pulls us up as we reach out to Him.

Every time I read about Peter I cannot help but ask, "How many people will allow themselves to be in such a position as Peter?" It is the kind of position where we can wind up screaming, "God, help me or I am dead!"

And that is exactly where God wants us. Unsión has been in such a position many times. But every time we are reaching up, crying for help, God miraculously shows up, and we suddenly know we are exactly where we need to be.

INTERVENTION

days after the
unsión building
burnt down

Once we made ourselves available to God's will, turned over our gifts to Him, pledged to fight any giants that came our way, and determined to embrace any change God brought us, we immediately started seeing a need for God's intervention.

As I walked through the remains of the Unsión studios, the acrid smell of burnt plastic and wires filled my nostrils. Computers, cameras and editing equipment were melted as if made of wax.

If not for the word I had received from the Lord about the fire not taking Him by surprise, I would have been overwhelmed with grief. Everywhere I looked were reminders of all the hard work, money and hours countless people had poured into Unsión. Much of what was given and built was now gone.

"Lord, we need a miracle," I prayed as I straddled twisted beams and stretched to step over black puddles of water.

"Pastor Bill," Eduardo Gonzales said, "we must go to the Catholic university. You aren't going to believe it."

"Believe what?"

"The team is working to get us back on the air," he said. "Maybe by tomorrow."

"Tomorrow?"

"Yes, it's true. Tomorrow. The Catholic university has loaned us their auditorium until we get back on our feet."

As Eduardo and I drove to the university, he told me what happened in the minutes after the firefighters extinguished the fire.

"We gathered in the street and sang 'Thank You, Lord,'" Eduardo said. "Then we prayed and thanked God for all He was doing and going to do."

When it was safe to do so, our employees began picking through the debris, salvaging any equipment that looked usable. The day I arrived, our team was at the university constructing a temporary base of operations where we could broadcast.

That was the first miracle. The second came in the form of public interest. Without prompting from us, national media outlets throughout Ecuador swept into Cuenca to cover the fire.

Suddenly, Unsión was taking center stage in the nation's consciousness. We were painted as an underdog network just trying to bring something positive to the airwaves. Sympathies and donations began rolling in. We even received a commendation letter from the vice president of Ecuador for putting family-friendly programming on the air.

The third miracle happened only two days after the fire when we were back on the air using a hodgepodge of equipment.

The attention and financial boost gave us the momentum we needed to press forward. But what we did not know was that God was just beginning to show us that He had everything under control.

As word of the fire spread, people came to our aid. Randy Hurst, director of AG Relief, promised to walk alongside us financially as we rebuilt. Without that commitment, I doubt Unsión would be here today.

Donations from Ecuadorians and Americans poured in as well. Within six months we found a new building, took a leap of faith to purchase it and moved in. Even though insurance covered less than one-third of the $600,000 in damage, by the end of 2006 we were in a new building twice the size of our previous studios. We were able to double our staff and double the number of programs produced.

"All things — even bad things — help make us better," Eduardo Gonzales told me one day.

As I think about the fire, I think of another miracle. In 10 minutes the fire swept through the studios. Several of our workers were trapped in a courtyard at the rear of the building. Miraculously, no one was killed or injured.

We thank God for all of His provisions. And each morning when I pray, I thank Him for showing me miracles — no matter how taxing they may prove to be.

At Unsión
we believe work should be fun

Every effective organization has a vibe that is palpable. At Unsión we have learned that building employees up, encouraging their enthusiasm, and releasing them to be creative is really just good business.

If you do not believe me, just step into an office where employees are ripped down regularly, their creativity is thwarted, and they are not empowered to do their jobs. The chill you will feel will take your breath away. Such an office might as well have a sign on the wall that says, "Fun is forbidden. Anyone caught enjoying what they're doing will be punished."

For energy to be effectively contagious it must be communicated. Leighton Ford, author of *Transforming Leadership* (InterVarsity Press, 1993), suggests nine imperatives we can learn from Jesus about communication.

1. *Know where you're heading.*

2. *Know your source and identity.*

3. *Know the power of language.*

4. *Know your audience.*

5. *Know your craft.*

6. *Know your timing.*

7. *Know your point.*

8. *Know where your responsibility begins and ends.*

9. *Know your enemy and know your ally.*

We can decide how to respond to our mission and the circumstances that challenge that mission. A response of positive, faith-fueled energy makes all the difference in the world at Unsión.

I once asked a seasoned missionary, "What is the secret of becoming a good missionary?"

"Have fun," he said. "Whatever you do, do not stop having fun."

I have used his idea to rudder my life and ministry. When I am having fun in my marriage, my marriage is energized; when I am having fun in ministry, my ministry is energized. Yes, marriage, ministry and life itself include very hard and sacrificial times. I'm not calling on anyone to live in denial and claim that pain or illness or loss is fun. However, most of us can still find those opportunities to live with a sense of fun and joy, even in the midst of un-fun circumstances.

Hugh Downs, the former veteran television journalist, once said, "A happy person is not a person in a certain set of circumstances, but rather a person with a certain set of attitudes."

There is a parallel between focused energy and God's call on our lives. In 1984 I had the opportunity to travel to Mexico with my wife and daughter. I was so touched by the need and poverty that I sensed a pull to Latin America. But it was vague. Was it the need, the romantic idea of missions, frustration with my present position, the thrill of adventure? Fortunately I was reading the book *The Man Who Could Do No Wrong* (Tyndale House Publishers, 1982) by Charles Blair. Blair's conclusion noted there are many compelling needs in life; however, the only valid reason for a Christ follower to move is a divine call.

I believe I had a divine calling to the mission field. I also believe God called me to start Unsión.

"Blessed are those who hunger and thirst for righteousness, for they will be filled" (Matthew 5:6).

Hunger and thirst for eternal dividends energize the staff of Unsión. We believe we are part of a great and eternal plan that will help transform families for generations to come. I often tell our staff that we have teamed with God for His purposes. That knowledge drives us forward with holy confidence.

In the end, the successful ministry is the one that harnesses the energy and resources God provides and directs both toward lost people He was willing to pay the ultimate price to save. I pray Unsión will somehow communicate to each of our viewers how priceless they are to God.

INVESTMENTS

Enrique and Juan had been attending our church for a few months after finding Christ. One Sunday afternoon, after I had preached a sermon about one's personal responsibility to share Christ with others, the two friends were in the local market having lunch.

While Enrique and Juan ate their traditional meal of pork skin and montepillo (hominy and eggs), Enrique felt a tug at his leg. He turned to see a young street beggar at his side with long, sad eyes.

Enrique told the youngster he had spent the last of his money on the meal he was eating but would gladly share that meal. I think of Peter's statement to the lame man at the temple: "Silver and gold have I none, but such as I have give I thee ..."

"Have some of my food!" Enrique offered.

After the meal, Juan and Enrique invited the boy to our evening service. We were greeting one another at the close of worship when Enrique introduced me to his newfound friend. The little guy was so small I whisked him up in my arms.

As the people began to be seated I took the boy to the platform with me. I asked him his name.

"Segundo," he replied.

"How old are you, Segundo," I asked.

"Nine," he said, "but I might be 10."

Knowing he had nowhere to stay that night, I asked him if he would like to become part of our church family. He nodded his head affirmatively.

"How many would like to invite Segundo to become part of the 'family?'" I asked our people.

A huge smile spread across Segundo's face as the congregation began to applaud.

After church, Segundo went home with Enrique. Over the next weeks he moved around the congregation, staying in one home then another.

One evening after a Sunday service I asked Segundo where he would be spending the night. His gesture implied he had no idea.

"Well," I said, "you can come home with me tonight." We had a youth event at church Monday morning, and I knew I could drop him off there to hang out with the kids.

When we got home I decided to wash his clothes and let him wear something of Leah's to bed.

I first sent him up for a shower. I had to show him how it worked and to be careful with the hot water.

"Hot water," he said enthusiastically. "I've never had a hot shower before!"

After he had spent some time in the shower, I knocked on the door and told him it was time to finish up. I returned a few minutes later to insist he get out, only to find the door locked! I had to practically threaten his life to get him out of that shower.

Leah was only a couple of years older than Segundo, but her clothes swamped him. Her sweat pants hit him just under the armpits; the sweatshirt came to his knees.

CHANGE count on it

We went to the kitchen to eat a cheese sandwich Connie had prepared and placed Segundo's clothes in the washer just off the eating area. A washing machine in the early '90s in Ecuador was an absolute luxury. Segundo had never seen one in his life. The women in his world take their laundry to the Tomebamba River, part of the headwaters of the Amazon. They beat the clothes against the smooth rocks near the banks, a laborious task.

Our washing machine, because of the few clothes in it, got off balance and began to knock violently. Connie adjusted the clothes, and the washer continued to function without incident. After the cheese sandwich and prayers we were off to bed. We had prepared Segundo a place on the couch.

The next morning we were up early to head to church to meet the youth. When we arrived at church Segundo promptly jumped down from the car and made his way to the building. As he approached some of the youth, he put his hands on his hips and proudly said, "Had a hot shower last night, and guess what? Pastor Bill has a white box with a lady inside who washes your clothes really hard!"

Segundo eventually returned to his home in Cumbe, the same place we had planted a church a couple of years earlier. I have seen Segundo off and on over the years. On one occasion I asked him how he was doing and how old he was.

I thought it was funny when he replied, "I am 24, but I might be 25."

Nothing spectacular happened when I took Segundo home. He had not won the lottery. He would encounter plenty of challenges in life after that evening. But that night was one more expression of the turning point Segundo reached when he discovered a group of Christ followers who looked for ways to tangibly communicate to him the priceless value we knew he possessed.

I have experienced that kind of turning point.

transformers

When we were pastors in Lexington, our family had endured the loss of two children. I went through a season when my ministry felt fruitless. It did not matter how I prayed, how I prepared a sermon, how fervently I tried to connect with our people, I still felt ineffective.

In that state of pain and vulnerability, people's comments cut me to the bone. Being a pastor, you have to anticipate a certain level of criticism. It comes with the territory. But I felt every day was a fight I could not possibly win.

Then Pastor Rodgers stepped in.

I remember the day he took me out for coffee.

"Billy, let me tell you a story about a friend of mine," he said.

"Sure," I replied, politely but half-heartedly.

And then he began to tell me about a man he said I should meet. He talked up that man's natural gifts of serving, helping others, being in tune with God through prayer and sensitivity to the voice of the Spirit.

Who is this guy? I wondered.

"Billy," he finally said, "that man is you!"

A light went off in my mind and spirit. It was another turning point in my ministry and life. Someone believed in me! I realized I just needed to hear that someone thought I could do it.

I simply communicated that same message to Segundo. I passed on the gift I had been given. That kind of affirmation is the key not only to personal ministry, but also to any level of leadership. To inspire people to follow you, to commit themselves to your endeavor, to make needed sacrifices, you have to offer an inspiring mission. You have to create confidence and passion in them.

Your message does not need to be dramatic, but it does need to be meaningful. It simply needs to be a message of hope. One that the person can refer to when things get tough and the impossibility of their situation seems overwhelming. When a person has an experience like that to rest on, they can make it through anything.

At Unsión
we believe we can
expand the kingdom of God

The closest thing I had to a brother growing up was my cousin, Joseph Carl. He went by J.C., and every weekend we would hang out together. During the summers we would stay at each other's homes. As the old saying goes, J.C. and I were closer than brothers.

But after I married Connie, J.C. got married too and moved to South Carolina where he served in the U.S. Army as a military policeman. As with many great friendships, we eventually drifted apart, only staying in touch through our parents.

In 1977 I received a phone call and learned that J.C., 22 at the time, had brutally murdered three people. It did not seem possible. But while strung out on angel dust, J.C. and two accomplices went on a killing spree.

He was quickly condemned to death in one of South Carolina's electric chairs. A few months after his sentencing, he called and asked if I would come and visit him.

"Billy, can I just tell you the story?" he asked shortly after I arrived at the prison.

"Sure, J.C.."

"I just need to tell someone what happened."

He began going down the list of his crimes, telling me vivid details that sickened me. Several hours passed before he came to the end of his story. When he did, he looked me square in the eyes.

"Billy, I just need someone to forgive me," he said. "Will someone just forgive me? Because I can't forgive myself."

I told him Jesus would forgive him if he asked Him to do so. As we sat in the visiting area, I led J.C. to a relationship with Jesus.

"When they execute me, I want you here, Billy," J.C. said before I left that day. "Can you be here?"

"Of course."

On the day of J.C.'s execution, I was led with his mother and two younger brothers to a small building the guards called the Death House. It had just two cells, a room that housed the electric chair and a gallery for the witnesses.

Two large generators were brought over to the Death House to help carry out the execution. As we entered J.C.'s cell, I could hear the humming of the generators reverberating throughout the tiny building.

After I entered the cell, J.C. and I embraced and immediately started talking about our childhoods, his newfound faith, old girlfriends, brotherly fights and the Bible.

"Nanny always used to take us to church," he said of our grandmother. "Those were some good days."

After lunch, a guard came to the cell and told us we had one more hour left. To that point it was almost like nothing was ever going to happen — especially the death of my cousin. As the reality of the situation sank in on all of us, each of us searched for the right words to say. Several minutes passed before J.C. broke the deafening silence.

"Billy, what do you want me to tell Nanny?"

I was not expecting such a question. As I pondered that question, it felt as if heaven settled in on that little cell. I was speechless.

"What do you want me to tell her, Billy? Come on."

"Tell her I love her, I'm doing well, I'm serving God and I'll see her again."

As I finished my sentence, a thought flooded my mind. "J.C., would you do me another favor?"

"Anything, Billy."

"When you run into my two children, Billy and Katie, would you tell them I miss them terribly? And that one day their mom and I will hold them again."

"I promise you I'll do that."

My encounter with J.C. was one of those moments that marked a difference in my life. From then on I decided to live for heaven's sake. No longer would I allow myself to be caught up in the things or affairs of this world — even the good stuff.

It is a lesson we champion at Unsión. In addition to that, I also tell our staff to:

Laugh. If you are not laughing, it is probably because all the junk of this world is robbing you of your joy.

Love. I like this saying: "Looking back, I have this regret: that too often when I loved I did not say so."

Give. Winston Churchill once said, "You make a living by what you get, but you make a life by what you give."

In the Death House the guards moved the family to another room as they prepared to transport J.C. to the electric chair. After they had shackled him at his wrists and ankles, they escorted him out of the cell.

Over the public address system I heard a guard say, "Dead man walking."

As J.C. made his way towards the death chamber, our eyes met. He smiled at me, and then raised his thumbs like the Fonz used to do on *Happy Days*. I read his lips: I ... will ... see ... you ... again.

That is something we would say at Unsión to every one of our viewers. Because that is our hope, — to see every viewer in heaven.

TRANSFORMED

Napo, a man in our church, sold oranges for a living. Not an easy job. To collect oranges to sell, Napo had to travel over a 14,000-foot pass that winds through the Andes Mountains before descending into the Amazon jungle where he would meet with the Shuar Indians and purchase the oranges.

After he had loaded his truck with oranges, he would drive back up the mountains, through the treacherous pass and back to Cuenca. There, he would sell his oranges in fruit stands and at little markets.

After he returned from one trip to the Shuar, he recounted to me how he had shared his faith with the Indians.

"In a little Shuar village I shared with the men about how I have come to know Christ and met God in a very personal way," he said. "I told them how that had transformed my life."

When Napo finished telling his story, the chief of one of the villages told him he wanted him to come to the village and share his story with all the women and children too.

"Pastor Bill, you need to come with me."

"Just tell them the story you told the men," I offered.

"It's too late, Pastor," Napo said. "I told the chief my pastor would come back with me. He said that would be fine. Now you must come to the Shuar with me and tell the village people about Jesus."

A few weeks later Leah and I joined Napo and loaded up our vehicles with generators, the *Jesus* film, candy, bedrolls, food, water, Bibles and a projector.

We set out early in the morning for our eight-hour trek. After leaving the cobblestone streets of Cuenca, we hit the dirt road and made our way to the pass. The road is thin and snakes through the mountains. Sometimes it feels as if the truck is barely clinging to the road. With no guardrails in some spots and 1,000-foot drops at many turns, it's a white-knuckle experience.

As we made our way down that perilous road, I prayed regularly that we would not plummet off the edge. We stopped in Logrono, unloaded our vehicles and rented some pack animals for the second leg of our journey, which would take us deeper into the jungle on horseback.

After we loaded the animals with our gear, we began following Napo down a muddy trail to a village that had never known modern conveniences. Two hours later we arrived in tiny Narjem-Paimi.

Our arrival was an unusual event for the Shuar. Some of them had never seen a white person before. Most had never seen the kind of gear we were carrying. We might as well have been aliens dropping out of the sky.

As Napo introduced Leah and me to Lucio the village chief and elders, a Shuar girl snuck up behind me and rubbed the hair on my arms. When I looked down at her, she scurried to her mother and asked, "Is he a monkey?"

We laughed, and more children came out to see the white monkey. Since we suddenly had a captive audience, I told Napo we would have children's church first. We started by playing with the kids and telling them simple Bible stories. As we did, the children's mothers gathered around us and listened intently to what we were saying. Members of our team started ministering to them.

life change

Then the men started coming in from their hunting and gathering trips. Other members of our team started ministering to them. Within an hour almost everyone in that village was engaged in our makeshift church.

By 6 p.m. it was getting dark, so we hung up a white sheet, rigged a light bulb and then fired up the generator. As the generator and the light bulb came to life, everyone was amazed. For many of the Shuar, it was the first time they had ever seen a light source other than fire and the sun in their village.

The generator hummed, and people from other villages stepped out of the forest and joined us. Like moths, they all seemed attracted to the light. The communal hut we were using to show the film had standing room only, and people peered through the doors and holes in the walls that served as windows to get a look.

As the *Jesus* film played, many of the Shuar were riveted to the screen. Some of them I would learn later had never seen a picture, let alone a moving one before.

As the film was coming to an end, I heard the chief, Lucio, and some of the elders speaking. Not sure what was wrong, I approached them and asked if I could be of any help.

"Pastor Bill, do you happen to have any more of those film

things?" the chief asked.

"I do."

"We want to see another film."

I obliged them and put in another film we had. It was not as long as the *Jesus* film, but by the time the second film was done three hours had passed since I had started the projector.

"Pastor Bill," Lucio, the chief, called. "We would like to watch the *Jesus* film again."

"Again?"

"Yes, we don't want to aggravate you or anything, but can we see that first one again?"

I looked at my watch. Our day had started at 4:30 a.m., and it was now well past 11 p.m. I was tired, but more than willing to do anything for these dear people.

"Sure, we can watch it again."

After we watched the *Jesus* film for a second time, I gave an invitation to receive Christ.

"How many of you tonight would like to believe in the Lord Jesus Christ?"

It was the very first time anyone had ever made a presentation of the gospel in the village. The thought that there are millions of people who have never heard the gospel should motivate every follower of Christ to share his or her faith whenever the opportunity arises.

"How many of you would like to trust Jesus as your Savior?" I asked. "If you do, please raise your hand so I can pray with you."

Every hand in the hut went up. I felt inspired and thankful for the opportunity to lead so many wonderful people to the Lord. I also could not help but marvel at the fact that God would use me to do such a thing. He was not using me because I had a plethora of great gifts; He was using me because I was available.

As I prayed the sinner's prayer, the Shuar Indians repeated the prayer. It was a moving moment as I watched close to 125 people secure their eternity in Christ.

The next morning as we prepared to leave, the entire village came to see us off. Our team passed out the New Testaments and the candy we had brought.

"This is the Word of God," I said. "This is what God wants to say to you."

Lucio insisted on traveling with us to our cars that were parked two hours away. He was such a kind man, so thankful we had come that I wanted to do something extra for him.

"Lucio, I want to do something for you," I said. "What do you need? I want to give you something."

As the words left my mouth, it dawned on me that I was making an ill-advised offer. To Lucio, I was the richest man he had ever known. He could ask for anything, and I may or may not be able to provide it for him.

Suddenly Lucio stopped walking and grabbed my hands. Instantly, I felt very nervous. What was he going to want?

Would I be able to provide what he requested? The worst-case scenarios were racing through my head.

"Pastor Bill," he said honestly. "Send us someone to teach us the Word of God."

Lucio's words flabbergasted me. Here I am with all my stuff. If truth were known, if some rich guy were to ask me what I wanted I would have told him I wanted more stuff.

"Teach us the Word of God," Lucio continued. "Send someone who can teach us the Bible."

I nodded and promised to do so. As the journey continued, I could not help but think that the Shuar had an inside line to God that I, with all my comforts, must have somehow neglected or lost in pursuit of all the material things I was racking up.

For years after that visit, I prayed that God would raise someone up to go to the Shuar Indians and teach them about Jesus and His marvelous love. Though it would be years in the making, God did send someone with a heart for the Shuar. Actually, He sent two people: our daughter, Leah, and her husband, Joil.

Today, if you go to the village of Narjem-Paimi you will find a little Assemblies of God church very close to the spot where we showed the *Jesus* film. If you venture out from the village in almost any direction, you are bound to run into one of the 45 additional churches that have been planted in the area or the Bible institute where Shuar are preparing to plant and pastor churches.

visionaries

There are approximately 100,000 Shuar Indians, and 80

percent have yet to hear the gospel. Joil and Leah are intent on training pastors to reach every Shuar with the gospel.

Leah made that trip with me when she was 12 years old. A few weeks after returning from the trip she told me she wanted to win a nation for Christ. Even then I knew she was embracing a battle she could not win in her own strength. She needed God to help her embrace the vision before her.

God has a vision for every one of His followers. The vision might be leading your family, friends or co-workers to Jesus. It might be embracing a call to ministry or starting a food program for those in need in your community. The vision might be opening your home to foster kids.

Like my daughter told me when she was 12, we need to do the same with our vision.

For almost a decade, Unsión has been my vision. In that time I have seen lives changed. Thousands of people have committed their lives to Christ, in part because Unsión has ministered to them. That's why we exist — to see changed lives.

Eduardo and Ximena Gonzalez are an example of changed lives. Eduardo had become a drunkard and carouser. Ximena knew of Eduardo's drinking but had no idea that Eduardo was seeing someone else.

But through a series of events she discovered his indiscretions and confronted him. The marriage seemed irreparably harmed, but Ximena started attending our church at the invitation of a business acquaintance.

"I continued to go because they sang songs and I felt at home," Ximena told me. "When I went home, I told Eduardo that he was not the number one love in my life. Jesus is now!"

Eduardo told her she was crazy and refused to leave his life of sin.

"When I heard her say she loved Jesus, I knew what kind of fight I was getting into," Eduardo would later tell me.

Ximena started a Bible study in their house. Her countenance changed, but Eduardo kept falling deeper into sin. When he would leave to party with friends, she would tell him she was praying for him and that she loved him.

Feeling confused and guilty about his wife's change of heart, Eduardo held onto the life he was living. But one night he agreed to meet with me. Eduardo and I became friends, and he began to see that he could have fun without getting drunk.

One night Eduardo met with me and told me all his problems. I looked at him and said, "I can't help you."

Eduardo looked at me sideways and said, "I've just wasted all my time telling you all this, and you can't help me?"

"No, but Jesus can."

Soon after, Eduardo committed his life to Christ and asked Ximena for forgiveness. In the following years I discipled Eduardo and he grew in the Lord. His and Ximena's marriage improved greatly. Today, he works for Unsión as our executive president.

That's what Unsión is all about. Changed lives and giving people a glimpse of the Greatest Hope they will ever know.

Now, that's change — the kind you can always count on.

At Unsión
we believe all things are possible with God

Miguel, 14, spent his days on the streets of Cuenca, doing his part to support his impoverished family whose home is in the slums.

The sad truth is that there are thousands of families like Miguel's in Ecuador and millions of them throughout the world. The vast majority of children in Ecuador live like Miguel. Due to families facing the daily challenge of trying to meet the bare necessities to stay alive, there is no way to go to school or receive any form of education or training. It's a vicious cycle that is passed from one generation to the next.

On the streets, kids like Miguel face more than hunger. They have to survive in the shadows and deal with the dangers that lurk there. Daily, children must avoid the hooks of human trafficking, prostitution, gangs, crime, drugs, homelessness and for some — even death.

Despite the odds we believe that Unsión can be God's hand extended to these kids. In other words, we believe that all things are possible!

One day Miguel wandered (or should I say was led by the Lord) into a place of rescue called PANITA. It was there that it was quickly recognized that Miguel had a special talent for acting. To bring awareness to his and countless other kids' plight, Miguel agreed to be a part of a documentary that would expose the injustice and needs of street kids like him.

In the documentary viewers saw how Unsión's partners could change Miguel's life. Through his story viewers saw firsthand how:

- Unsión has led the way in the battle to salvage broken lives like Miguel's by providing education and training through Latin America ChildCare.

- Unsión reaches entire families by providing family counseling at Un Buen Consejo (Good Advice).

- Unsión TV is able to bring awareness to the masses through the medium of television.

- Unsión's faithful prayer and financial partners help kids like Miguel learn the skills and earn the certified degrees that have the power to pull them out of poverty.

Why Unsión works

Unsión is a network of influencers committed to impacting the worldwide Hispanic community with positive family values. This vision is expressed through three objectives:

COMMUNICATION: Unsión Television reaches into the lives of families with stories of ethics, virtue and faith.

•Unsión's programming provides an alternative to other broadcast networks that are in opposition to needed Christian values.

•Unsión's programming has proven to the public that commercially viable programming can reinforce a positive, family-friendly Christian view.

COMMUNITY: Unsión reaches into Hispanic life through Un Buen Consejo.

•Services include counseling, family workshops, evangelistic commercials, education and literature.

•Un Buen Consejo has registered more than 100,000 contacts since its inception in 2003.

•Un Buen Consejo also trains Christian volunteers to be the human face to the message of "Jesus loves you," as told through Unsión's community and school workshops.

COMPASSION : Unsión's compassion ministry is expressed through PIEDAD.

- PIEDAD works hand-in-hand with local churches and Latin America ChildCare.
- PIEDAD reaches local communities through 14 schools, representing more than 2,000 students.
- PIEDAD makes a difference in both the lives of the children and their parents.
- PIEDAD brings positive change to the community through a holistic education that is Christ-centered.

partners wanted

Unsión cannot change lives on its own. We need your prayer and financial help.

Will you help continue Unsión's many outreaches?

Will you join hands and heart with Unsión to reach and to change the lives of other kids like Miguel?

Will you give financially and pray for Unsión?

for more information or to become a partner please contact us at:

Bill and Connie McDonald
P. O. Box 198032
Louisville, KY 40259
bill.mcdonald@agmd.org

Unsión Donations:

Unsión International
AGWM account #693941
1445 N. Boonville Ave.
Springfield, MO 65802

Web Sites:

Unsión International *www.unsion.org*
Communication: Unsión Television *www.unsion.tv*
Community: Un Buen Consejo *www.unbuenconsejo.org*
Counseling (Spanish) *deseo@unbuenconsejo.org*
Compassion: Latin America ChildCare *www.latinamericachildcare.org*

Appendix
Unsión TV overview

Unsión Television is a family-friendly, Spanish-language television network founded in Cuenca, Ecuador, in 2003. Our programming is carried on 53 cable systems in Ecuador and numerous outlets across Latin America.

Our wide variety of family-friendly programming reaches a broad base of viewers, many of whom would never watch traditional religious programming. Our programming provides an alternative to other commercial broadcast networks that adhere to a worldly viewpoint and present programming filled with sexual innuendo and violence. Our programming has proven to the public that they can enjoy quality programming without sacrificing godly values.

Through our Un Buen Consejo counseling service, which is promoted every half hour on our network, we have touched the lives of tens of thousands of people who have made commitments to Christ, and many are now members of local churches. Our satellite signal reaches from the southern tip of South America to the Canadian border, and includes a beam that reaches most of Europe. In everything we do at Unsión Television we adhere to a biblical worldview and solid Christian values. We believe that by telling the story of God's love for the world we can be an instrument of change in people's lives. For more information, including program descriptions and our broadcast schedule, visit our Spanish site at www.unsion.tv.